Make Your CD-ROM Work!

How to Survive a Bad
"Out-of Box" Experience

Make Your CD-ROM Work!

How to Survive a Bad
"Out-of Box" Experience

Bob LeVitus • Ed Tittel

Random House

Acknowledgments

We'd like to thank anyone and everyone who has ever performed technical support for CD-ROM titles, or who ever will. Special thanks to Kenneth Knotts, former Apple Support guy, currently Power Computing Corporation Tech Support Lead. An incredible debt of gratitude and appreciation to James Michael Stewart, for research, writing, and development assistance, especially for the PC part of this book. It's safe to say we couldn't have done this book without you!

Contents

Introduction

If you're standing at the counter of the CD store looking at this copy of Making Your CD-ROM Work, wondering if you should spring for it, the answer is,
"absolutely." We promise that this book is, by far, the
fastest, easiest, least expensive way to get any CD-
ROM title to run on your PC or Mac.

In a moment we'll talk about what you get with
this book, but first, let's look at some of the things
this book will help you avoid:

- Long distance charges for calls to tech support.
  (We've done it for you!)

- Listening to bad music-on-hold while the long
  distance charges rack up. (Ditto. In spades.)

- The frustration of getting inaccurate or bad
  advice once you are connected to a live person.
  (We went to great lengths to confirm that the
  advice in this book is both accurate and easy to
  understand.)

- The (usually bad) advice of so-called friends.
  (Just follow our simple and easy-to-understand
  step-by-step instructions and ignore what everyone else tells you.)

- The pain of a problem that occurs (of course)
  after the vendor's support lines are closed.
  (Unlike tech support at most vendors, this book
  is open weekends and late at night.)

- Bad documentation. (Documentation says: "Check your CONFIG.SYS file." We show you how and explain what that means.)

And much, much more. Simply put, using this book is almost certain to solve your CD-ROM problems faster and easier than any other way.

Who this Book is For

This book is for any PC or Mac owner with a CD-ROM drive. That's pretty broad. More specifically, it's written for computer novices—the less you understand about your computer, the more helpful this book will be to you.

Even so, mega-power-users will almost certainly discover stuff they didn't know. We spent literally hundreds of hours reading bulletin board messages and UseNet newsgroups, and talking to technical support staffers at popular game companies, all so you wouldn't have to. Thus, even the most powerful of power users may learn a thing or two.

The bottom line is this: This book costs about the same as a single long distance call for support. But unlike a call to tech support, this book will almost certainly solve your problem. And unlike some calls to tech support, this book is easy to understand and available 24 hours a day.

Don't get us wrong. A call to tech support can sometimes be a joy. Many of the CD-ROM publishers we called had really first-rate people manning their phones—they were absolutely wonderful to deal with. Others were less wonderful, with only automated answer lines or support by fax available. Most of them, even some of the good ones, put us on hold for at least a little while (some much longer than others). The point is, 9 times out of 10, the answer is here in this book, saving you a (possibly) lengthy long-distance call or fax.

So regardless of whether you're a rank beginner or a grizzled computer veteran, if this book can save you a single long distance call for support—and it will—it was a good deal.

How to Use the Book

Well, you could read it cover to cover (it wouldn't really take that long). But we suspect few of you will do that. So, here's our guide to using this book effectively...

The first thing to do is check the Table of Contents. Each chapter covers a particular aspect of multimedia computing. The chapters are relatively short, so you might want to read all the chapters that seem to apply to your problem before you continue.

If that doesn't solve it, try Appendix B. As you'll soon discover, *How to Make Your CD-ROM Work* is mostly a collection of questions and answers (or, more specifically, problems and solutions). In Appendix B, we've listed every question (problem) in the book, arranged them by topic, and cross-referenced them to other relevant questions. Give it a try.

If that doesn't do the trick and you're *still* having problems, try the comprehensive index at the very end of the book.

If you're still stuck after all of that, there's a good chance you have either defective hardware or a defective CD disc. You'll know when you've reached this point—it comes after you've tried all the solutions in the chapters, index, and appendices without success. If this happens to you, sad to say, you'll have no choice but to call the manufacturer of either your computer or the CD for replacement or repair.

One final note: Defective hardware or software is relatively unlikely though not unheard of. In almost any other situation, if you follow our instructions carefully, you'll be up and running and having fun again in no time at all.

Where Did Our Questions Come From?

In the process of researching and writing this book, we compiled the questions we answered from two primary sources:

1. By talking to the technical support operations at the companies listed in Appendix C: List of Contributing Vendors, and addressing their customers' most common queries and problems. It's amazing how consistent they were, from vendor to vendor.

2. By cruising the multimedia, CD-ROM, gaming and other forums, bulletin boards, and newsgroups to observe the online give and take between users and experts. Here again, we collected the most common questions and prepared the kinds of answers we think you, our gentle reader, can use best.

In fact, you wouldn't be wrong to think of this book as "The Greatest Hits of CD-ROM-Related Technical Support!" All we did was bring this information together into one place, to save you the time and aggravation of spending your life on hold, or of cruising the digital highways and byways for that one essential bit of information you lack.

About the Authors

Ed Tittel has been fooling around with CD-ROMs since the late 1980's, when he got seriously hooked on the Macintosh and the PC. Until 1994, he was a "moonlight writer," the co-author of four other books with Bob LeVitus, and numerous others, all focused on one aspect of the computer industry or another. Since mid-94, Ed's been out on his own as a full-time freelance writer, with a Windows help column with Bob LeVitus for **MAXIMIZE** magazine, and articles for publications like **IWAY, NetGuide,** and **Infoworld** on his recent list of credits. Mostly, he just wishes the phone would quit ringing long enough so he could squeeze in a few more rounds of Vortex!

Bob LeVitus got his first CD-ROM drive a long, long time ago, when he was the editor-in-chief of the seminal monthly **MACazine** (which he was until its untimely demise in 1988). Since 1989, he has been a contributing editor/columnist for MacUser magazine, writing the Help Folder, Beating the System, Personal Best, and Game Room. He has also written or co-written 17 computer books.

As the **MacUser** Game Room columnist, Bob has the opportunity to review 3 or more Mac games every month, and look at many more than that. He says, "It's a tough job. You have to really love your work. I *love* my work!"

Part I

The PC Side of the Multimedia World

Questions to Ask Before Problems Occur

1

In this chapter, we will address a number of issues that are best dealt with *before* you try to install any new system components, be they software packages or hardware products. If you have to ask any of the following questions during a product's setup, you obviously did not read this chapter first. Shame, shame, shame. Learn from our experience, and avoid the unsightly messes that might otherwise result!

Q1: The setup asks for information about my computer, like memory size, CPU speed, COM ports, etc. Where can I find this information?

The easiest way to locate this information is to look it up in the computer information file (CIF) that you've safely stored near your computer manuals. What, you don't have a computer information file? Well, it's about time you made one. Here's what's involved:

A computer information file has every conceivable tidbit of information about your computer that you can find. This includes:

- type, brand and model of your computer, including type and speed of CPU (e.g., 386/33 or Pentium/90).

- types, brands and models for all peripheral equipment (e.g., printers, modems, tape drives, CD-ROM player, etc.).

- configurations for all expansion cards (be sure to include IRQ, MemBase, DMA settings, etc.—at least, all those elements that apply).

- sizes for all floppy and hard drives.

- list of installed software, versions and serial numbers.

- directory structures for all hard drives.

- paper and floppy copies for all configuration and .INI files, especially AUTOEXEC.BAT and CONFIG.SYS for DOS and WIN.INI and SYSTEM.INI for Windows.

- a functioning boot disk (test it to make sure it works!).

- page of technical support numbers for each product.

- warranty cards and information.

- notes of spacing, layout, empty expansion slots, and empty drive bays.

- an error and solution log.

- a date on everything.

This list is not exhaustive, so if you can think of other types of useful information, put that in the file, too.

Some of these items are self-explanatory, but we

will walk you through the others to insure you get the right info.

Capturing Configurations

Knowing your computer's model and type is important. If you have the receipts and manuals that came with the equipment you should be able to look this up. If not, your computer can tell you (by the way, don't assume that what is written on the computer's case is accurate or correct).

You'll need to run a simple program that examines your system, and provides a detailed report. Microsoft ships a nice little program with MS-DOS and Windows, that many people don't even know exists. This program is called MSD.EXE (short for "MicroSoft Diagnostics program").

If you have MS-DOS 5.0 or Windows 3.1, or any higher-numbered versions of either program, you already have this program. Get to a DOS prompt and type **MSD<ENTER>**. Once MSD has examined your system, you'll need to print out its report. To do this, select the Print command under the File on the title-bar menu. After it prints, take a few minutes to familiarize yourself with the information this program retrieves. (You can use a highlighter to mark the important sections, like the IRQ Setting, I/O addresses, and basic computer info).

Your listing of the configuration for each of the expansion cards in your system is another significant part of the Computer Information File. This includes your video card, I/O cards, disk controllers, game cards, sound cards, SCSI controllers, and whatever else you've got.

You'll also need to gather up the manuals for each card. For each one, look through the manual to determine its configuration and make a list of the allowable and default settings.

> **Note:** if your system is under warranty, you should not open the case. Please consult the place of purchase to have them help you obtain this information.

When you record configuration information, be sure to include required software settings, such as exclusion of specific memory blocks from memory managers (this is common for many video cards). The more you know about the way your system is supposed to work, the better you'll be able to keep it working!

Swinging in the Directory Tree

It's easy to create a printout of your computer's directory structures, as long as you own a printer. But you should look at the tree for each drive before printing it, because some of these trees can be extremely long. Here's a peek at what a directory tree looks like:

```
Directory PATH listing for Volume
SLAVE_D_420
Volume Serial Number is 381D-16FB
C:.
+---DOS
+---WIN
|   +---SYSTEM
|   |   \--WIN32S
```

```
|     +---MSAPPS
|     |    +---MSQUERY
|     |    +---GRPHFLT
|     |    +---MSINFO
|     |    +---SHEETCNV
|     |    +---PROOF
|     |    +---MSGRAPH5
|     |    +---ORGCHART
|     |    +---ARTGALRY
|     |    +---TEXTCONV
|     |    +---EQUATION
|     |    --WORDART
|     \--TWAIN
|          \--CALIBRAT
\--WIN_APPS
     +---LVIEW
     +---WINZIP
     +---FMTBAR
     +---FMSTEPUP
     +---PLUGIN
     +---QUICKENW
     |    +---TUTORIAL
     |    \--BACKUP
     +---MSOFFICE
     |    +---SETUP
     |    +---MS-BTTNS
     |    +---EXCEL
     |    |    +---EXCELCBT
     |    |    +---EXAMPLES
```

You, too, can create a similar tree view on your own computer. Get to a DOS prompt, and type: (change the drive letter for each hard drive you want to look at)

```
cd c:\
tree /a
```

Obviously, you'll need to capture this information

7

to a file to make any use of it; so type:

```
tree /a >list.txt
```

This captures the output from the tree command into a file named LIST.TXT located in your current DOS default directory (because you've set your default to the root of the C: drive in this example, that file would reside in that drive's main directory, C:\).

You can use any text editor in DOS or Windows to view this file and print it. Watch out, because it can be dozens of pages long. If you are truly brave and love to kill trees, you can pipe the tree information directly to your printer: (if your printer isn't attached to **LPT1:** but is attached to **LPT2: or LPT3:**, change the last entry in the next line to reflect the proper assignment).

```
tree /a >lpt1
```

You can use this tree structure to list the software installed on your system. Don't forget to list patches, drivers and helper programs that you may have installed or added that do not have directories (or subdirectories) of their own.

To get a complete list of every file on your hard drive you can add the **/f** option to the tree command. CAUTION! This command option causes the output to be voluminous, and it may be hundreds of pages long. This option is recommended only for file capture, not for printing. To see what we mean, use the following command line:

```
tree /a /f >list.txt
```

Backing Up for Safety's Sake

Making a backup of your startup and config files is easiest from a DOS prompt. You will need a blank floppy, format it if needed (format a:). From DOS, type:

```
cd c:\
copy autoexec.bat a:
copy config.sys a:
cd windows
copy win.ini a:
copy system.ini a:
```

Substitute the desired floppy drive letter for **a:**.
Substitute your chosen directory name for **windows**.

A boot disk can be an invaluable rescue tool. Make more than one and carry it with you at all times (if you're paranoid, never leave home without it). To make a boot disk from DOS, type:

```
format a: /u /s
cd c:\
copy config.sys a:
copy autoexec.bat a:
```

Substitute your floppy drive letter for **a:**.

Next, test your new boot disk. Leave it in the floppy drive and reboot or reset your computer. It should read from the floppy during the boot up; it'll work a little slowly but should otherwise boot the same as from your hard disk (unless you forget to update it as you delete subdirectories. Using an outdated boot disk can cause the system to look for drivers on the C drive that no longer exist—keep your boot disk up-to-date). If your test is successful, make a few more copies of the floppy, label them clearly, and store them in a safe place.

The Errors and Solutions Log

An error and solution log can be a very useful tool. Take time to write down any problems or errors that occur on your system more than once. After you solve any problem, write a brief description of its diagnosis and cure. If the same problem ever recurs, you'll know what to try first.

The CIF Is a Good Tool

Now, you have a computer information file. It can be a useful tool as you and your computer learn and grow together. But if you fail to keep it up to date, it will become useless. Every time you add software or hardware to your system, take notes and make changes to the CIF. Label new information with its installation dates; label old information with change dates. As the old saying goes: "An ounce of prevention beats a pound of cure," or better still: "A moment of preparation saves a millennium of reconfiguration."

Q2: I ran out of disk space during the installation. What can I do about it?

If you discover you don't have enough disk space after you've started installation, you've failed to properly prepare. Before you install any software product, read the box and the installation instructions. Be sure to verify that you meet the product's minimum installation requirements.

Insufficient disk space requires a multistep remedy:

1. Determine if the installation program has altered any startup or system files. If so:

   - Restore the files from your backups (see why you made them?).

   - If you don't have backups, check to see if the installation program automatically made backups that you can restore from.

 Note: *backups often have files extensions like: .BAK, .OLD, .001, .B~K, or three letters that match the name of the product for instance sound programs sometimes name backups .SND.*

   - When no backups exist, try to edit the files yourself (use a text editor). Be sure to match them to the printouts of the files you made. Without backups or printouts of the configuration and startup files for your particular system, it will be a difficult if not impossible task to restore these files to their original state.

     Knowing that every system on the entire planet can have different setup configurations, there are no general statements we can make about what should or shouldn't appear in your startup files. If you don't have backups or printouts of your startup files, you're basically out of luck!

2. Locate files and directories added during installation; carefully remove them. Be sure to remove only those files you're sure were added; don't delete anything on the drive prior to installation. This task will be made easy if you use the handy printout of the directory tree structure that we recommend you make in the answer to Q1.

3. Read the installation instructions. You should be able to determine how much hard drive space is required for installation.

4. You may opt to remove other software packages you no longer want, in order to make room for the new one. Before blindly deleting a software package, check for an uninstall utility, or for instructions about how to deinstall the software. This is not purely straightforward, especially where Windows is concerned.

5. Before you try to reinstall the new software, be sure to back up your system files. You might also want to make and leave a copy of these files on your hard drive. One approach is to use the **COPY** command to create a new file with a different extension.

 Hint: *Use your initials to identify your private copies.*

Repeat the following command for every file you want to back up (but replace "nnn" with your initials):

```
copy autoexec.bat autoexec.nnn
```

Q3: The software says I have an incompatible product installed on my computer, or that I'm lacking a specific required product. How can I be sure?

First, reread the instructions and requirements for the software (if you read them carefully the first time, you may never encounter this problem). All software that requires specific hardware or software should clearly list these requirements on its packaging, in its installation guides and in its manuals.

If you don't own a required product, you will not be able to use the software. If you do own the product, it is probably misconfigured or improperly installed. Refer to the product's manuals to determine the proper setup.

If you own an incompatible product, you have two basic choices:

1. You can decide not to install your new stuff, and stick with what you've already got.

2. You can decide to deinstall the incompatible stuff, and then install the new stuff instead.

After verifying your configuration, if your new software still doesn't recognize the product it requires, pick up the phone and give the vendor's tech support a call. If a software package fails to recognize a properly configured system, there may be a few screws loose that only tech support knows how to turn. Why not ask them?

Q4: What are "minimum requirements?"

Minimum requirements define the basic system configuration that allows a software package to function. If your system fails to meet any one of these minimum requirements, chances are good (or should that be bad?) that the software won't function properly. Installing software on a system that doesn't meet minimum stated requirements is just asking for trouble.

Often a manufacturer lists recommended configuration, as well as a minimum configuration. Wherever possible, configure your system to meet or exceed the recommended setup; that way, you'll realize the best possible performance. Because minimum configurations identify those set ups where the manufacturer is sure the system won't work, you're usually better off meeting or exceeding the recommended configuration instead.

Q5: I updated my software, and my old configuration, setup or data files are gone. What happened?

Unfortunately, too many software packages—including upgrades and patches—aren't designed to save and adapt previous option settings. In order to circumvent this problem, you should locate and back up all configuration files, option settings, or other aspects of a program's environment that change according to your settings. These files may have extensions like: .INI, .CFG, .DAT or .BAT. If you make a back up before installing anything new, you can restore those files if they're overwritten or damaged during the upgrade process (or if you decide you like the old version better).

Warning: *If you fail to back up before instal-lation, you will have to manually reconfigure your software, and edit all affected system files by hand. If you lose data files, they'll stay lost.* **Never, never, never** *keep the only copy of a data file on your hard drive. Don't even keep the backup on the same hard drive. Whenever possible make a floppy or tape backup of your data files. The only way to restore data correctly is to restore data that has been backed up properly, or taken from an accurate, correct copy of that stored some-where else.*

Q6: I started to install new software but it crashed during installation, or I aborted during installation, or it finished installing, and now my computer doesn't work the way it did before. What can I do now?

When your computer fails to operate as it should, this is usually due to a change in the system's config-uration or to its startup files. The easiest remedy is to restore those files from the backups you made before installing the software in the first place.

If you failed to back up before starting the instal-lation, check to see if the installation utility was friendly enough to make backups for you. These nor-mally have file extensions like: .BAK, .001, .B~K, or .OLD.

If you don't have a back up, here are a few more avenues to pursue before you give up:

- Look in the installation manual for a list of

changes made to the configuration files. Some user-friendly software companies clearly inform you about all changes they make to your system. Use this information to edit out the changes. Some companies try to help you out, and add a comment line with information above or below the line they've added to INI files at installation (e.g., ";next line added by: XYZ Corp").

- Call the software company's technical support line. You'll need to have your computer information file handy when you call. If you don't have a CIF, do your best to answer the questions the tech support people will ask about your system. Let them explain their restore procedures to you; maybe you'll get lucky!

If restoring startup files doesn't remedy the situation, you may have one of the following problems:

1. Some portion of your hard drive has been deleted. Using the DOS **DIR** command, check the directories and files against your printout from the **TREE** command. If you have missing files, try using **UNDELETE** to restore them. If the data hasn't been disturbed, you should be able to successfully restore deleted files. If you're unable to restore files and you don't have a backup to restore from, you may need to consult a waste disposal company (by the time you finish kicking your computer it won't be good for much else).

2. Your hard drive has been formatted or repartitioned. Usually these actions aren't reversible. If you have a backup, you'll have to use it to restore your system.

The only reliable way to recover from this type of problem is to have a backup. Let's say it all together now: BACKUP! BACKUP! BACKUP! Equally important to the practice of backups is to test the integrity of the backup. Performing a verification after a backup will insure that there is data to restore!

A backup is your friend. A backup will save marriages. A backup will reduce stress and increase world peace. Not having a backup is just like not having a backup. With a valid backup, you can recover from any and every problem caused by any and every installation utility. Even if your computer has a warp core breach, you can restore a backup to a new computer and get back to life as you know it. The alternative is, as they say, "Unthinkable!"

Q7: Where are my backups? & Where is my CIF?

These should be the most stressful questions you should ever have to answer. If you don't have them, the stress will convince you to create them for future use. If you do have them, locating these items will be the only stress you should experience.

SUMMARY

In this chapter, we've tried to prepare you to deal with installation of just about any kind of hardware or software on your PC. If you do your homework in advance, create a backup of your system, and maintain a current computer information file, there's not much that the computer industry can throw your way that should lead to total panic. If you're prepared, you can do it. So get prepared!

CD-ROM Drives— Compact Disc or Chaos Director?

2

In this chapter, we'll discuss problems and difficulties that you might encounter with your CD-ROM drive.

> **Q1: It worked before but it doesn't work now. What can I do?**

The first thing to try, every single time you encounter a problem, is to reboot your system. Exit all programs, turn off the power, count to 10, turn the computer back on, and then try using your CD-ROM drive again.

If your drive is external (in its own box, not built into your PC's case), be sure to turn its power off for a few seconds, too. If it still doesn't work on a second try, re-seat all the connections and power cables.

Before you give up on the CD-ROM player, try a different disc than the one that's giving you problems; if it's defective, it can make your CD-ROM player appear inoperative when it's working fine (but the disc isn't).

Computers are complex machines. Dozens of drivers and files may be loaded into its memory at any moment. Sometimes loading one file accidentally overwrites a driver. When this happens, devices or software programs can become unstable or cease to function. When this happens, your only recourse is to restart your computing session. Unfortunately, this problem occurs way too often in the most popular PC environment—namely, MS Windows.

If a restart doesn't cure your blues, it's time to start a little detective work. The first question to ask is: "Have you installed any new software or hardware since you installed the CD-ROM?" If you have, try removing it and retest the CD-ROM. You may have introduced a conflict with the new product. You will need to check your configurations and try reinstalling the new item. Or, you might try reinstalling your CD-ROM software instead (but if you do, check your new addition when you're done; there's a chance that it will be disabled now).

> **Q2: I can't read the disc directory, I can't run any of the programs on the disc, or the CD-ROM drive does not appear in the File Manager or as a DOS device. What should I do?**

Here is a list of possible culprits:

- There is no CD in your drive.

- The CD-ROM drive door is not closed.

- The CD in your drive is upside down.

- Your external drive doesn't have power or isn't turned on.

- The disc caddy is seated or inserted incorrectly.

- The disc tray is misaligned or not in all the way.

- The CD is for a different computer type (e.g., you're trying to read a Macintosh disc on a DOS PC).

- Try another CD—you may have a badly-produced or defective disc.

Q3: The drive doesn't appear to work. What can I do?

A dead CD-ROM player may be the result of many causes, ranging from a driver conflict or collision to a loose connection. The only way to fix your problem is to identify and correct the cause. Here are some things you should check:

1. Your CD-ROM's driver may not have loaded into memory. Reboot to allow the drivers to reload. If this solves your problem, you may have had a driver conflict or one of your drivers may have overwritten your CD-ROM driver. Reboot your machine, and see what happens. This will fix the problem in many cases, but if you are still having problems:

   - Reinstall your CD-ROM software and drivers.

   - Get out the manual for the CD-ROM. Using the manual and a text editor, check to see that the correct driver names are listed in the appropriate startup files. Edit where necessary.

2. You may be having a software conflict. One or

more programs may be trying to gain control of the CD-ROM drive at the same time.

- Be sure you're using only one CD-ROM program at a time. If you have an audio CD player loaded, exit the application before opening File Manager's CD-ROM icon. You may be causing these collisions by misusing your CD-ROM software.

- It's also possible that one software package may have loaded a second CD-ROM driver that conflicts with your usual driver. You'll need to read the manuals for both the CD-ROM player, and the new software, to determine which driver you should be using. If you discover an errant driver, try to remove it. If it's in the AUTOEXEC.BAT or CONFIG.SYS you can delete the line or remark it. If it was installed under Windows, you will need to use the Drivers application in the Windows Control Panel group or edit the appropriate .INI file.

 Note: *to remark a command add* **REM** *at the beginning of the line; this prevents the command from being executed, but makes it easy to restore if you ever need to.*

3. Another culprit can be hardware-related. If you've changed or added to your system's hardware setup, you may have inadvertently created a conflict. Undo your changes and retest the CD-ROM.

If your changes caused the conflict, reconsider its necessity or usefulness. If you still need or want the change, reconfigure your system's hardware to eliminate any conflicts. Remember, most interface cards each have an IRQ and an I/O address; so be sure to check them all. They must all be unique, or you'll have problems.

4. If your CD-ROM drive is a SCSI device, check to see that all the connections in the SCSI chain are secure. Next, be sure that each device on a single SCSI daisy chain has a unique ID number, and remember that the SCSI interface card also has an ID number—usually ID#7. While you're at it, check for proper SCSI termination; where more than one or two devices are in a chain, the first and last devices on the chain must be terminated. The order of the ID numbers on the chain is not important, but they must be unique.

Q4: I just changed discs, why do I still see the directory for the previous disc?

Under Windows File Manager, you'll need to refresh the listing by pressing **F5**, or you can use the Window Refresh command from the menu bar.

If this doesn't bring up the correct disc directory, or you aren't working within Windows, you're probably experiencing a caching problem. To fix this, reboot your computer to reset the cache. If this problem recurs frequently, check your CD-ROM and systems manuals for the available caching options. You may need to change the cache refresh rate (the interval at which the contents is recreated) or the size of the cache (the amount of data it can hold).

Q5: My CD has dirt, finger prints or dust on the data surface. How should I clean it?

First, let's discuss how to prevent this from happening again:

- Always store CDs in jewel boxes or nonscratch CD sleeves. **Never, never, never** lay a CD down unless it is inside a jewel box, sleeve or caddy.

- Always hold a CD by its edges. You can even put a finger in the center hole if you have small hands.

- Keep your computer area clean and free of food and drink.

- Keep monkeys and farm animals under close supervision when using your computer.

To clean a disc:

- Use only a soft, lint-free cloth. Never use a towel, paper cloth or even your shirt because these materials are abrasive and can scratch the disc. Use a record-cleaning, CD-cleaning, or gold polishing cloth.

- When cleaning, use radial strokes from the center to the outside edge. Never use circular motions; if you do scratch the disc while cleaning, radial scratches can often be corrected by the CD-ROM reader (see Q6).

- Only use a CD-approved solvent or cleanser. Spray a disc and let it sit for a few minutes, but NEVER RUB OR SCRUB!!! Using radial strokes, wipe off the cleanser. Repeat this until the disc is clean.

- Dust can be removed easily with a can of compressed air. Be sure to get a dust removal can, and not the freeze spray for gum removal. Use short bursts aimed from the center to the edge.

- There are little machines designed to clean CD-ROMs, most of these are designed to provide the radial cleaning action and include a cleansing fluid. Use these with care and caution.

Q6: AARRGGHH! My disc has scratches, is there any hope?

Scratches can make a disc useless. However, a few scratches don't automatically make it unreadable. Most discs are designed with an ECC (Error Correction Code). ECC is a method of recording the data redundantly on the CD; this allows a CD-ROM drive to reconstruct the data which is unreadable under a scratch, from the surrounding data. ECC can overcome some surface flaws, but preventative care is always preferable.

There are a few options to repair scratches, but these should be employed cautiously, and they are listed in order of the level of damage they can repair or damage they can cause if misused.

1. CD polish can remove small scratches. This product is available at most audio CD stores or through music magazines.

2. Liquid metal polishes, like Brasso, can fill in small scratches. Use these sparingly!

3. Toothpaste, yes toothpaste, a brand made for

polishing teeth. Using your finger and a small amount of toothpaste, gently polish away the scratch using radial reciprocating strokes. Use warm water to rinse the CD. Use CD polish to smooth the scratches the toothpaste caused. Be sure that you understand you will be making scratches to fix a scratch.

4. Commercial/professional plastic polishing techniques. This is the method of using fine abrasive paper and liquid polish. Most plastic supply companies have these materials and can give you detailed instructions. This is only a last resort.

Q7: My CD-ROM seems to read discs poorly. Can I fix this?

Yes, this is often caused by a dirty lens. First try using compressed air to dust the lens. Then try using a soft Q-tip and rubbing alcohol to gently shine the lens. Some audio CD stores sell lens-cleaning systems, these may also be employed on your computer's CD-ROM player.

Try other CDs in the drive. If you still experience poor disc reads, call the CD-ROM manufacturer or return the product to its place of purchase; you may have a damaged drive. If it's still under warranty, you may be able to obtain a replacement at low or no cost.

Q8: What is an MPC level?

An MPC level is a standard published by the Multimedia PC Marketing Council. These are standards for multimedia hardware platforms—in other words, these standards define the level of multimedia performance a certain hardware configuration can consistently supply. Software manufacturers use MPC levels to identify the minimum compatibility requirements for their software. Currently there are two MPC levels, Level 1 and Level 2.

	MPC Level 1	MPC Level 2
CPU	386SX	25 MHz 486SX
RAM	2M	4M
Drives	1.44M 3.5" floppy 30M hard drive	1.44M 3.5" floppy 160M hard drive

CD-ROM	150K/sec transfer
	    rate
	1 sec or less
	    seek time
	10,000 hours MTBF
	Mode 1 capability
	
	Subchannel Q
	CD-DA outputs
	Front-panel volume
		300K/sec transfer
		    rate
		400ms or less
		    seek time
		10,000 hours MTBF
		CD-ROM XA ready
		Multisession capable
		Subchannel Q
		CD-DA outputs
		Front-panel volume

Audio Card	8-bit DAC and ADC
	Linear PCM
	    sampling
	22 KHz sampling
	    rate for DAC
		16-bit DAC and ADC
		Linear PCM
		    sampling
		44.1 KHz sampling
		    rate for DAC

	11 KHz sampling rate for ADC	44.1 KHz sampling rate for ADC
		Stereo input and output
	Microphone input	Microphone input
	Synthesizer	Synthesizer
	Multivoice	Multivoice
	Multitimbral	Multitimbral
	6 melody / 2 percussive	6 melody / 2 percussive
	Mixer: 3-channel input Stereo output	Mixer: 3-channel input Stereo output
Video	VGA	VGA /w 64K colors at 640 x 480
Input	101-key keyboard 2-button mouse	101-key keyboard 2-button mouse
I/O	9600 bps serial port Bi-directional parallel port MIDI port Joystick port	9600 bps serial port Bi-directional parallel port MIDI port Joystick port
System	Windows with Multimedia	Windows 3.1 Extensions

Be sure your system has at least the minimum requirements for your chosen software's MPC level.

Q9: What is a cache, and can I use one with my CD-ROM?

A cache, also known as a disk-caching program, is a utility that stores recently-used information in RAM. Your computer can reaccess this information much more quickly from RAM than by rereading it from a drive. Using a cache is useful for some-but not all-multimedia packages. Most packages will clearly state whether or not to use a disk caching program. If a package doesn't mention caching, test it with the cache turned on and then with the cache turned off, to determine which setting delivers the best performance. The most noticeable speed differences occur during long audio and video sequences.

One caching program that you may already own comes with MS-DOS; it's called SmartDrive. But only the most recent versions of SmartDrive—those included with MS-DOS 6.2 and later versions—can cache CD-ROM drives.

SmartDrive may be loaded in AUTOEXEC.BAT or at the command prompt. To enable CD-ROM caching, be sure to include its drive letter as one of the command's parameters. Here's an example (substitute your drive letters as needed):

```
C:\dos\smartdrv a- c+ d+ 2048 128
```

If you place this line in your AUTOEXEC.BAT be sure to place it after the drivers for your CD-ROM are loaded, otherwise it will not recognize the CD-ROM's drive letter. (For more detailed information about SmartDrive, please refer to your DOS manual.)

If you need to disable CD-ROM caching, drop the CD-ROM drive letter from the command line and add **/u** before the RAM sizes. This will force SmartDrive to ignore the CD-ROM for caching purposes.

Many other caching software utilities are available, and they all seem to offer comparable performance. Each utility will have a different set of command line options and parameters, so read its manual carefully. We've had good luck with Helix Software's Multimedia Cloaking cache, and with PC-KWIK's caching software.

Q10: What is a buffer and how is it used?

A buffer is a memory area on an I/O device where information is stored until the CPU can process it. Most good CD-ROM drives feature a data buffer of at least 64K, but some have 256K or more.

 Watch Out! *Most CD-ROM packaging calls the device's hardware buffer a cache. Don't confuse this with caching utilities like those we discussed in Q9. The larger the buffer, the faster and more consistent the data flow will be from your CD-ROM player to your computer's CPU. You will notice good buffer size and usage most during long audio and video sequences.*

If your buffer is sufficiently large, you'll only notice fascinating graphics and sound; but if your buffer is inadequate, you'll notice skips, stutters, lines, blurs and shakes during playback. Very few CD-ROM drives can increase their buffer sizes, but a small buffer can sometimes be offset by a good caching utility. Otherwise, you'll want to buy a newer model CD-ROM player, with a larger cache.

> **Q11: I bought a new Quad or Hex spin CD-ROM drive, but my programs don't seem to run any faster. Why?**

The increased speed of the new high spin drives has yet to be exploited by CD-ROM manufacturers. Most software packages are based on MPC Level 2; therefore, they only require a 300KBps transfer rate. On a triple spin device, video and audio quality is often increased, but rarely will the software take full advantage of the 450KBps transfer rate. Generally, most software on the shelves today won't run any faster on a Hex spin than on a triple spin device.

That is not to say that no high speed CD-ROM software packages exist, because they do. With these specially-designed packages you'll need drivers that can handle the increased data throughput. A quad spin device is the minimum we'd recommend for new CD-ROM player purchases today, because we expect that most new software will require quad speeds or better by the end of 1996.

Sound

3

In this chapter, we answer questions regarding sound for both DOS and Windows environments. Most of the questions, unfortunately, have more than one potentially valid answer. This will sometimes mean a little trial and error testing on your part to figure out which potentially valid answer really is valid.

As always, when trying to isolate problems by trial and error, reboot and retest your system each time you make a change. If you do this before continuing on to the next step, and things don't work, you'll be able to eliminate this particular solution as a fix. If, on the other hand, you change three things and your system is fixed, you'll be left wondering which of the three things really did the trick!

DOS

Q1: When I run my game, or its set up utility, my PC locks up. Why does it do this?

Lockups can occur under two different conditions:

1. There could be a conflict between the sound card's configuration and another component in the computer.

2. The initialization software for the sound card is incorrectly set, or the software configuration does not match the hardware configuration for the sound card.

Both of these situations are easy to fix. First, you'll need to know the configuration settings for all the components in your computer. [Please consult Chapter 1, Q1: The setup asks for information about my computer, like memory size, CPU speed, COM ports, etc. Where can I find this information?]

Your sound card must be configured so that it does not conflict with any other component in your computer. Refer to your sound card's manual to determine all the possible configuration options. Select the best set of options for your card, taking into account what's already installed on your system. Then, follow the sound card manual's instructions to configure the card to match.

After reinstalling the sound card, you'll need to rerun the sound card's setup utility. Be sure to match the software settings with the hardware settings (especially if anything has changed). If the sound card's software has a test suite or a diagnostics program, use it to verify that your configuration is O.K.

Now you can run **Setup** or reinstall the game. If you're prompted for sound card information anywhere during that process, be sure to enter the correct settings.

Note: *80–90% of sound card problems are due to improper interrupt (IRQ) settings. A sound card, as with all other PC hardware, must be properly configured before it can be properly installed in any computer. Rarely will a "fresh out of the box" sound card configura-*

tion work on a PC that already has other expansion boards already installed.

Note: Using the default settings for a sound card, or any PC interface card for that matter, is highly recommended whenever possible. Unfortunately, many programs (including some of our favorite games), are designed to work only with the default settings on a limited number of sound cards; worse, they usually have no configuration capability.

One default setting to watch out for in particular is for older Sound Blaster models. These older models used a default IRQ setting of 7, while newer ones now use a default IRQ setting of 5. Many programs have difficulty using IRQ 7 for sound; therefore we recommend that you set even older Sound Blaster cards to use IRQ 5.

Note: Many hardware products and software programs claim to be "100% Sound Blaster compatible." This is more often false than true: Be sure to fully test any so-called "compatible" cards, or software products, before taking them home (or better yet, get a money-back guarantee if you can't make it work on your system). Because most software products cannot be returned once they are opened, be sure that your hardware matches the requirements listed on the box!

Q2: I've reconfigured my sound card and checked it against the rest of my computer hardware, but my game still locks up. What now?

If you have reconfigured and the problem still exists, you may not have a sound card that is fully compatible with the software package you want to use. You will need to call the manufacturer's technical support hotline, and discuss your hardware with them. They may have a patch or an update that fixes the problem, or they may know about a workaround that can get you off the sidelines and back into action.

Note: Patches and updates may often be found on the Internet, on one of the on-line services (like CompuServe, AOL, or Prodigy), or on the manufacturer's BBS (if they have one). It's a good idea to check one or more of these resources out before calling Tech Support, because it can save you time and money waiting on hold to talk to a real human being (which is, alas, increasingly hard to do at most hardware and software companies these days).

Q3: My game runs fine, but I don't hear any sound at all, or I only hear sound effects, or I only hear music, or I can't hear any digitized voices. How can I get all the sound I'm supposed to?

First, check the volume settings on your speakers, and on your sound card. Also, be sure the speaker's power is on (if applicable) and that your speakers are plugged into the sound card. Not every software package requires the same volume setting, but all of them require access to working speakers!

Second, check your sound card's mixer software. This is usually a software program that's loaded by the sound card's installation utility. The mixer usually includes settings for left-right balance, gain, amplification, and output levels. Check to see that these are set to reasonable levels, and that all the channels are turned on (it's hard to get sound from a channel that's turned off).

Third, you may have an improperly configured sound card. This is similar to the problems covered earlier in this Chapter in Question Q1. If you follow the instructions in Q1, your problem should be easy to find and fix.

 Note: *There are many kinds of sound reproduction available from most sound cards, including FM synthesis, MIDI and digital. Only the 16-bit (or higher) cards can play two or more channels, or types of sound, at one time. If you have an 8-bit sound card, it probably can handle only one or two types of sounds. In order to hear all the possible sounds supplied by some programs, 8-bit sound card owners will need to upgrade their hardware. Since this will probably cost at least $80, you may want to ask yourself how important hearing "everything" is, anyway!*

Q4: My game runs OK, but the sound is jerky. Why does it start and stop while it's playing?

On some 8-bit sound cards, it's not unusual for sounds to pause occasionally while they're playing. Obviously this disrupts play (if not your concentration) and lowers performance. Start-and-stop sounds occur when your PC's CPU sends a large enough amount of information to the sound card to overtax its on-board RAM, or memory.

All sound cards have a limited amount of memory in which to process incoming information and output sounds. Once the sound card's memory is full, your CPU is forced to wait until more memory space is available before it can send the rest of a sound signal.

If you notice this phenomenon, please consider upgrading your sound card. Such pauses may also occur on slower PCs, or with software programs that aren't written to handle sounds separately from other functions. That is, a game may require an explosion sound to be complete before it scores points, instead of playing the sound while the scoring subroutine pauses for 1/4 second, and then adds up your score.

This problem is particularly acute for 8-bit sound cards, because they have a narrower data path (and can therefore accept less data in the same amount of time as a 16 or 32 bit sound card), and because they typically have less on-board RAM (which means they have less room in which to store arriving sounds). Either way, this contributes to the sometimes "herky-jerky" nature of the sounds you may hear. Alas, when this happens, your best recourse is a hardware upgrade.

> **Q5: The sounds that come out of my speakers are crackly and distorted. What can I do?**

First, check your connections outside the computer. Unplug and reconnect all of the wires that plug into your sound card. Look for damaged wires or bent connections. Check the connectors and make sure they're clean and straight, too.

Second, turn the volume on your speakers down, and up on the sound card or in the sound card mixer software, or vice-versa. One element in your sound hardware chain may be overpowering the next element in the chain (like the amplifier on your sound card and the external speakers, or the mixer volume and the amplifier, etc.).

Third, check your sound card's configuration [as we recommended in the answers for Q1].

Fourth, check your speakers using a radio or a WalkMan. Your speakers may be damaged; these symptoms can occur if you've pushed your speakers hard enough to damage their paper cones.

Fifth, return your sound hardware to the manufacturer or vendor, and exchange it for another. Manufacturing defects do occur and you may be the beneficiary.

Sixth, move to Vermont. We hear it's nice and quiet there!

Q6: When I installed my sound card's software it changed my AUTOEXEC.BAT and my CONFIG.SYS. I was told never to mess with these. What should I do?

Most of the leading sound card manufacturers have reliable installation utilities. They examine and edit your startup files to load their sound drivers properly and safely. As we discussed in Chapter 1: ("Questions to Ask Before Problems Occur"), you should always make a backup copy of your startup files before installing new hardware or software on your system. This will give you a way out if installation fails to result in a working system.

Most sound card software adds one or more of the following changes to your startup files:

- TSRs to control the sound environment
- environmental variables to handle configuration settings for the sound card
- run card diagnostics to verify that the settings match the software.

Q7: The setup utility for the sound card asks for an IRQ, an I/O address, the MIDI port address and DMA settings for my sound card. How do I scope these out?

As a rule of thumb: For every computer product, whether hardware or software, always read the installation instructions before you do anything else (especially before starting the installation process).

Your user's manual should explain your card's default setting and the options available for reconfiguring them. If you stick the card in straight out of the box, you've failed to verify those defaults against the rest of your system [see chapter 1: "Questions to Ask Before Problems Occur"].

If you've got the rest of your system's configuration documented already, you should be able to determine all the necessary information by scanning the manual's installation section. Usually, they'll list the configuration options in one or more charts. Hopefully, they'll even include pictures of the DIP switches or the jumper settings necessary to change the configuration. Don't worry, if you don't get it right the first time, the computer will let you know!

Windows

Q8: I can't get Windows to make any sounds. Why not?

Windows is an operating environment where there's a specific driver for every aspect of the computer; sound is no exception. It's quite possible to load the wrong driver, or possibly, the right driver with the wrong settings, or, even to find that there's no sound driver loaded at all. The Sound application located in Windows' Control Panel supplies a simple way to test your setup. This application features a **Test** button, so why not use it? It'll tell you right away whether Windows can provide sound with the current driver and configuration setup.

Since Windows is more often mysterious than otherwise, before we tackle the possible high-tech culprits, we'll eliminate the obvious suspects first. To begin with, make sure that your volume is turned up for your speaker(s) and for the sound card (if applicable).

If you can't find any speakers, or you don't see a sound card, your problems may go beyond mere volume—you may need to visit the local computer store and buy yourself some! Otherwise, check all the wires that connect the speakers to the sound card. Then restart Windows and test again. If you still hear only the sounds of silence, consider how peaceful your situation is: Do you really want to shatter that with a bunch of computer noise?

Now, let's move on to the technical stuff:

1. Open the **Control Panel** and the **Sound** application. Be sure that the check box marked
   'Enable System Sounds' has an 'X' in it. Restart
   windows and test again. See Figure 3.1.

2. Try reinstalling the sound card's Windows software and/or its Windows drivers. This procedure should be explained in the hardware's
   user manual. After reinstalling these items,
   reboot, start Windows and test your computer
   again (lots of testing going on, eh?)

3. You may need to update your drivers. Check
   with the manufacturer, or one of the on-line
   computer services like AOL or CompuServe, or
   look for those drivers on the Internet.

Note: *Some Sound Blaster compatibles aren't.
We recommend that you stick with well-known
and well-serviced hardware. Often, the drivers
for a third party sound card will conflict with
software designed for the original product.
Likewise, software written for the original*

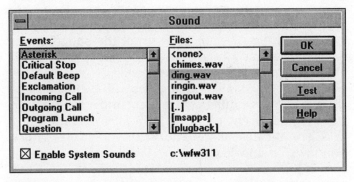

Figure 3.1 Sound Application

*product may not work with a so-called com-
patible sound card. But before you give up on
a clone sound card, please look for updates or
driver patches. They're free, but replacing the
hardware costs money.*

**Q9: When my system plays a sound, Windows
freezes or reboots. Why?**

This is nearly always a driver conflict, but alas,
driver conflicts come in many flavors. A driver can
conflict with a sound card's configuration, or with
another piece of hardware (or at least its configuration). A driver can conflict with other Windows programs, or when two drivers try to access the same
hardware concurrently. All of these things are bad,
but some of them are easier to fix than others.

First, you'll need to verify your sound card's configuration (go back to the answer for Q1). You may
need to reset it to the factory defaults and start over,
or if you have your system fully documented, you
might be able to pick other settings that don't conflict with other components on your system.

Second, you'll want to reinstall the sound card's
software, especially any Windows-specific items. If
the program offers an Uninstall utility, run that first,
before you reinstall; this may be sufficient to clean
up accidental conflicts. Also, remember to back up
your Windows environment (at least SYSTEM.INI and
WIN.INI, because installation can sometimes muck
Windows up unbelievably).

Third, look in the **Control Panel's Drivers**
application. Check the names of the drivers listed

there. Some sound cards use one driver, some use many, but usually the relevant driver will be labeled with the sound card's type or product number (or its name will be listed in the user's manual). See Figure 3.2.

Use the **Setup** button to view more information about the highlighted driver. Be careful not to change any settings in the **Setup** window unless you are certain that those settings need to be altered.

Note, too, that removing a Windows driver can be dangerous. You can cause other currently working programs to fail if you remove a driver they rely on. If you locate a driver for another product which you do not own or that you have removed from your computer, you may opt to remove it. Take the precaution of writing down any information you can find about this driver, just in case you need to reinstall it later on. This may even warrant calling the manufacturer's technical support line for help, if you can't find any information to help you through this process.

Fourth, locate any updated drivers or patches for the product that you are using. Many companies distribute these by BBS, on-line services, or even by regular Mail. You can call the company's tech support line, or go looking for yourself if you have access to an on-line service.

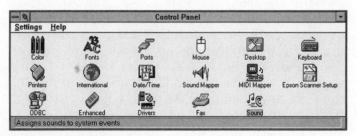

Figure 3.2 Control Panel

Misc:

Q10: I have an internal CD-ROM and a sound card. I should be able to play music CDs through my computer, but I can't hear any music. Why not?

Unfortunately, to let a CD-ROM play audio CDs through your computer, you need to purchase an internal audio cable. This little wire is rarely included in a CD/Sound card package, but can be purchased for only $10 or so at most retail computer outlets. This audio cable connects the internal audio output of your CD-ROM to the internal audio CD input on your sound card. If you already have such a cable, the problem may not be hardware related (at least, if the cable is properly installed—check that first).

Under Windows, you also need an audio CD player application. Most CD-ROM or sound card packages come with one of these applications, but if not there are plenty of shareware versions available. Furthermore, you need to have a CD Sound driver loaded in the drivers section of Control Panel (see Figure 3.3).

Finally, be sure that the sound card software is properly installed. You need to check the user's manual for the necessary installation instructions.

Under DOS, you need a DOS audio CD player program. These applications are usually bundled with the sound card, but DOS shareware versions abound as well. If you have the application installed but still can't get any sound, please work your way through the following steps:

1. Check the volume on your speakers, sound

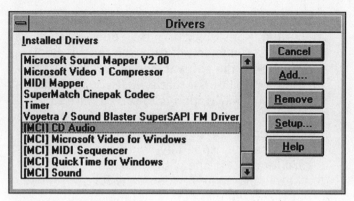

Figure 3.3 Drivers

card and CD-ROM.

2. Check the sound card's software mixer levels.

3. Reconnect all external connections, then check the internal connections.

4. Verify the correct configuration of the sound card and that these settings are reflected in the sound card's setup or boot-up utility.

Q11: I've covered everything mentioned in this chapter, but I still have sound problems. What else can I do?

Fortunately or unfortunately, there is a never-ending list of solutions to computer problems. Here are a few more to consider:

- Some software programs are not configuration-friendly. This means that some software packages, especially games, won't work with any configurations other than the Sound Blaster default settings. In our research for this book, over 10% of the software we examined had this limitation built-in. If that's what you're dealing with, your only option is to reconfigure to match these defaults, and change the configuration of other computer components like IRQ, MemBase, etc. Hopefully, you have a compatible card (or at least one with emulation modes). If all else fails, write the company for your money back, and tell them you can't make your system work with their product.

- Many graphics-intensive programs, especially games, require unique memory configurations, video and sound handlers, controllers and drivers. These packages usually require a boot disk that completely bypasses your standard boot-up files. If you have a nonstandard sound card, you may find yourself hand-configuring startup files to make things work. With such packages, as with any software, always read the installation instructions carefully. Often clues and troubleshooting tips for this software is written in plain English right on the page in plain view. All you have to do is read it!

- Call technical support. Some software companies have 1-800 numbers for tech support; if so, call these first. Some companies limit your access to free technical support to only 3 calls or 90 days. To keep your costs down, you'll want to be aware of this (it will be written near the phone number or on the product's warranty page).

    If a company has an 800 sales number but a long-distance tech support line, try calling the sales line and asked to be transferred. [Often, the sales department and tech support are in different buildings, cities, or states.] Most local computer retail outlets have tech support lines or can refer you to local or national tech support operations. Don't give up, thousands of people have had the same sound problems you're having; the fix may be just a phone call away!

Here's our final sound solution, one that you should consider if performance or compatibility problems plague you continually: Think about purchasing a new sound card. If you do, be sure to pick a solid name-brand product. Look for features like "stereo", "wavetable", and "16 bit" at a minimum; other great features are "MIDI", "DST", and "Qsound". Whatever you pick, make sure you get a money-back guarantee if it won't work on your system (and even then, pay with a credit card so you can get your money back from the credit card company, if all else fails).

We hope your system is sounding off nicely by now. If not, go back to the beginning and try again!

Memory—Can You Remember RAM? 4

In this chapter, we'll discuss problems and difficulties that you're likely to encounter with your PC's memory. Improper memory configuration is a common problem for many multimedia software packages, especially for DOS-based games. Unfortunately, finding the right solution to memory problems isn't always easy. Here, we'll point out some of the "obvious suspects," and give you the tools you need to ferret out and overcome the most common memory-related difficulties.

> **Q1: When I start installing or when I try to run a program, I get an error that states that I do not have enough conventional or base memory. How can I fix this?**

DOS PC machines may have up to 640K of base or conventional memory. Drivers, TSRs and other programs are often loaded into this area during bootup. If too much stuff gets loaded into this conventional memory area, other software (like your game, or other program) won't have enough room to run. The tricks here are to keep as much of this 640K memory region as available to programs as possible, and to find ways to take advantage of other RAM outside the conventional memory area.

Most programs will function fine when 550K of conventional memory is available after boot-up. But a system with only 550K of base memory available is either (a) poorly maintained or (b) has way too many drivers, TSRs, or other software loaded into conventional memory to be optimally configured. It's not unreasonable to expect a well-tuned PC to have between 580 and 620K of RAM available for programs after it's finished booting up. If yours has significantly less (550K or less, to be more exact), you may want to examine your configuration to see if there are some obvious candidates for memory relocation exercises.

Software installation guides usually list how much base or conventional memory is required for a program to run. Because these numbers are usually conservative estimates, you should always try to have more than this minimum available to the program you're trying to run!

It's easy to check how much conventional memory you have available on your PC. You can use MEM.EXE, a memory reporting utility that's prepackaged with DOS (version 3.X or higher). To run MEM, simply type MEM<ENTER> at any DOS prompt. Here is some sample output from the MEM program:

Memory Type	Total	=	Used	+	Free
Conventional	640K		22K		618K
Upper	187K		165K		22K
Reserved	384K		384K		0K
Extended (XMS)	19,269K		2,289K		16,980K
Total memory	20,480K		2,860K		17,620K

Total under 1 MB	827K	187K	640K
Largest executable program size		618K (633,008 bytes)	
Largest free upper memory block		15K (15,728 bytes)	

MS-DOS is resident in the high memory area.

This system's largest executable program size is 618K. In other words, there is 618K of conventional memory left to run programs in after boot-up is complete.

In order to free additional conventional memory (if your column listing under the Free entry for Conventional memory is too low for the program you want to run), you must move stuff out of the 640K conventional memory area. When it comes to freeing up additional space, you have two basic choices: [1] don't load any modules, drivers, programs, or TSRs that aren't absolutely necessary or [2] if they're necessary, try to load them somewhere other than in conventional memory. By taking advantage of Upper Memory Blocks (UMB) and High Memory Areas (HMA), many items that might otherwise consume conventional memory can be relocated, thereby conserving whatever memory they would ordinarily consume.

Note: *Until recently, the terms High Memory and Upper Memory were used as interchangeable terms. This is not correct: "Upper Memory" should only be used to refer to the area between 640K and 1M, whereas High Memory refers to all memory above the so-called "1M high-water mark."*

Note: *There's another confusing memory term that also needs clarification: LOADHIGH (a DOS MEMMAKER command) or loading high*

(a descriptive term for how software is loaded into DOS memory). To "load high" is to place a module into upper memory (into the UMB's between 640K and 1M) not into high memory. To make things a little more difficult, some software vendors have recently introduced tools to load certain modules, like a special version of the Microsoft MSCDEX CD-ROM driver, into high memory (e.g., Helix Software's MultiMedia Cloaking package).

UMBs and HMAs may be used only by means of a DOS memory manager. If you have a vanilla DOS system, EMM386.EXE and HIMEM.SYS are your built-in memory managers. While they can do an adequate job of managing your PC's memory, there are numerous third-party memory managers available that are much better at handling UMBs and HMAs. These include Quarterdeck's QEMM, Qualitas' 386 to the Max, and Helix Software's Multimedia Cloaking.

In order to free up conventional memory, it's a good idea to try the following activities (in the order indicated):

- Be sure to **back up** all of your startup files, especially CONFIG.SYS and AUTOEXEC.BAT before attempting any changes. In fact, it's a good idea to back up your whole system any time you plan to make major changes (and installing a memory manager certainly qualifies in this regard).

- If you're using only the memory utilities supplied with DOS, run MEMMAKER.EXE to optimize your startup files (see Q3 on how to use MEM-MAKER.EXE). MEMMAKER will examine your startup files and your system, take measurements of your memory usage and then modify your startup files to improve your memory layout. If you don't have the proper memory utilities loaded, MEMMAKER will add them for you. Once MEMMAKER has finished its job, be sure to test your software with this new configuration to make sure everything works.

- If you're using a third party memory manager, check the manual for a memory optimization utility. You'll want to learn how to use it, and then run it to relocate drivers, TSRs, and other memory-consuming elements into UMBs. For example, Quarterdeck's QEMM includes a utility named OPTIMIZE that does an excellent job of optimizing your startup files automatically.

- If you're using a program that imposes special configuration requirements on your system, you'll probably want to create a boot disk that loads only those modules required to run that particular software (see Q2 for boot disk creation). This is generally more efficient than optimizing your system for a single piece of software (and keeps you from having to reoptimize for other software, too).

- If you're running a vanilla DOS system, and you've tried all of the suggestions above, but have realized no significant increase in conventional memory, you'll need to invest in a good third-party memory management program. We recommend Quarterdeck's QEMM or Helix Software's MultiMedia Cloaking. With these, we've achieved 634K of free conventional memory on several of our test systems. Believe us, it doesn't get much better than that!

If you're able to increase your conventional memory beyond the minimum recommended by the software, but it still fails to function, work through the rest of the suggestions in this chapter before you call tech support. It's possible that you may be experiencing another kind of memory error that's acting like a conventional memory error. Until you've eliminated this possibility, a call to tech support will only take you through the exercises we're about to suggest, so you might as well do them on your own.

Q2: The software instructions for building a boot disk didn't work or I didn't understand them. How should I create a boot disk?

Creating a boot disk is simple, if you follow these directions:

1. Reread the installation instructions for the software. Be sure to notice its memory requirements, and any mandatory memory manager settings. Make sure you're not violating these restrictions.

2. Make backup copies of your CONFIG.SYS and AUTOEXEC.BAT files; for security's sake, make backups to your hard drive and onto a floppy. That way, if your hard drive is affected, you can still retrieve the data from the floppy.

3. Format a diskette and make it bootable. From the DOS prompt, use the FORMAT A: /S<ENTER> command. Label this diskette clearly as a boot disk for the specific program (e.g., "Rebel Assault Boot Diskette for MS-DOS 6.22").

4. Edit CONFIG.SYS and AUTOEXEC.BAT using a text editor to comment out all drivers that aren't needed. To comment out a driver (or any other statement) simply type the letters REM at the beginning of any line, followed by a space. REM stands for remark, and it instructs the computer to ignore each line that begins with REM.

   Start by removing drivers for hardware that won't be used by the software including things like: fax/modems, scanners, or extra SCSI devices. You may also opt to take out antivirus, screen-blanker and reminder pop-up type programs.

   Try to remove anything you don't think is essential to the operation of the software. Generally, you'll need to retain memory managers, sound drivers, SCSI utilities and mouse drivers. Pretty much anything else can usually go, however.

 Note: *Be sure to remove any calls to execute programs like Windows, menuing systems, disk scanners, and the like.*

5. Optimize your system using MEMMAKER or a third party memory manager optimization utility. (See Q3 regarding MEMMAKER usage or consult the manual for your utility.)

6. Reboot and test your software.

   - If it functions, copy CONFIG.SYS and AUTO-EXEC.BAT to the floppy you formatted.

   - If it fails to operate:

     - Try removing more modules. Go back to step 4.

     - Try adding or removing NOEMS or some similar parameter to or from the memory manager. You may also need to add or remove an EMS memory size, try 1024 and multiples. (See Q3 & Q4 regarding expanded memory) Go back to step 4.

- Try adding the parameter RAM to EMM386.SYS to allow DOS to use UMBs. If you're using EMM386, you can add a line that reads DOS=UMB to give DOS control over the free upper memory area EMM386 is not using for drivers. Go back to step 4.

- Try removing any disk caching soft-ware such as SmartDrive. Go back to step 4.

- Some software requires its own propri-etary memory manager. If so, you'll need to REM the lines that load your memory manager. Doing this may cause the rest of your modules to load erratically. You may also need to remove any special load instructions that your third-party memory manager might have added.

```
DEVICE=C:\QEMM\LOADH1.SYS /R:1 /SIZE=28976
C:\SCSI\ASPICD.SYS /D:ASPICD0
```

Should be changed to:

```
DEVICE=C:\SCSI\ASPICD.SYS /D:ASPICD0
```

Go back to step 4.

7. Once you've achieved success or suffered ulti-mate failure, you'll need to restore the original CONFIG.SYS and AUTOEXEC.BAT files to your

system. Be sure to reboot to verify that your system has returned to normalcy.

8. Go get a stiff drink, if you need one.

If you've worked through our 12-Step Program, or rather, 8-Step Program, you've done everything reasonable—and even a few unreasonable things—to create a working boot disk. If you're unable to do the impossible successfully, you'll have earned the right to call technical support and give them a hard time!

Q3: The software requires EMS. How do I provide it?

EMS stands for Elapse into Memory Suppression, or at least it should. Expanded memory (EMS) and Extended memory (XMS) are the two names associated with the use of upper and/or high memory. The nerds who named these standards should be shot. These two words are the hardest to keep straight. At any time, feel free to throw your head back and scream! (Hey, it works for us...)

EMS and XMS are not actually different types of memory, but different methods for providing software with access to memory addresses above the 1M high-water mark. The exact details on how each works aren't important here, but it is important to know how to activate, manipulate and vary the sizes of these two types of memory. If you want to know the down and dirty details about PC memory, consult John Goodman's excellent book, *PC Memory Management,* Deluxe Edition (Que Publishing, Indianapolis, IN, 1994).

To activate extended memory (XMS) on a vanilla

DOS system, all you have to do is load HIMEM.SYS in the first line of your CONFIG.SYS file.

```
DEVICE=C:\DOS\HIMEM.SYS
DOS=HIGH
```

By loading HIMEM and using the DOS=HIGH command you will also decrease the operating system's usage of the 640K area by 75%. If you're using a third-party memory manager, loading its main utility usually enables XMS. But since not all memory managers work alike, consult the utility's manual to verify this.

To activate expanded memory (EMS) on a vanilla DOS system, all you have to do is load EMM386.EXE in the second line of your CONFIG.SYS file.

```
DEVICE=C:\DOS\HIMEM.SYS
DEVICE=C:\DOS\EMM386.EXE
DOS=UMB
```

Note: *you must load HIMEM.SYS first, in order to run EMM386.EXE*

EMM386 simulates expanded memory using extended memory, and allows extended memory to be used for loading programs and device drivers. When EMM386 is loaded without qualifiers (as in the preceding CONFIG.SYS example), EMS is turned on by default. Without a memory size limit parameter, EMM386 enables all XMS memory to be converted to EMS. Fortunately, EMM386 only converts XMS to EMS when it is needed, and returns its EMS memory back to XMS when it is no longer in use. However, you may need to specify a maximum limit to how much memory EMM386 can convert. To do this, change the line to read:

```
DEVICE=C:\DOS\EMM386.EXE 2048
```

This example sets a 2M limit to how much high memory can be converted to EMS. You can specify any amount between 64K and 32768K (or the amount of free extended memory). 4M (4096K) should be the largest number you'll ever need to use (unless you're fond of manipulating LARGE 1-2-3 spreadsheets).

 Note: *remember that there are 1024 bytes in 1K, and 1024K (1,048,576 bytes) in a megabyte.*

The DOS=UMB gives DOS control of the free space in upper memory made available to it by EMM386. You can further the use of upper memory by DOS by adding the RAM parameter to the EMM386 line

```
DEVICE=C:\DOS\EMM386.EXE 2048 RAM
```

or

```
DEVICE=C:\DOS\EMM386.EXE RAM
```

or

```
DEVICE=C:\DOS\EMM386.EXE NOEMS RAM
```

 Note: *If you're already using the DOS=HIGH command line, you can add the UMB declaration to that same line, like this:*

```
DOS=HIGH,UMB
```

Note: If you're using a third-party memory manager, you probably shouldn't use the DOS=UMB statement, since the memory manager probably handles UMBs itself. Also, there may be differences in the actual parameter syntax for third-party memory managers, so be sure to double-check the manual before making changes to a third party memory manager statement.

Q4: My software doesn't work with EMS; how can I turn it off?

If you're using EMM386.EXE, you'll need to change its statement in the CONFIG.SYS file to read:

```
DEVICE=C:\DOS\EMM386.EXE NOEMS
```

You can add additional parameters after the NOEMS command if they're needed. If you're using a third-party memory manager you'll need to consult its utilities manual for the proper syntax for turning off EMS.

Q5: I've got all the RAM required for this software but it doesn't function correctly (or work at all). What can I do?

The amount of required RAM that's listed on a software package usually represents the absolute minimum required. Just because you meet these bare minimum requirements, doesn't mean that things are guaranteed to work. The minimum may work on perfect systems in perfect situations, but we have yet to be so lucky. If your computer includes only 4M of RAM, you should carefully consider an upgrade to 8M. The resulting increase in speed and reliability usually outweighs the cost, especially if you're running MS Windows.

If your software won't work with your system, and it already meets the minimum RAM requirements, try working through questions 1–4. If none of these approaches provides a working environment for your software, you may need to call the vendor's technical support for a software-specific solution.

Q6: How can I use MEMMAKER to optimize my startup files?

MEMMAKER should be able to handle most of the configuration tweaking that's needed to optimize your memory usage. It's a powerful utility that's shipped with DOS that's surprisingly easy to use. To begin, get to a DOS prompt and type: MEMMAKER<ENTER>. Be sure that you're not already using a third-party memory manager before you run MEMMAKER. Otherwise, MEMMAKER will remove other memory managers and replace them with its own DOS utilities. If you are using a third-party product, use its own optimization utility instead.

MEMMAKER starts with a welcome screen; you can strike any key to continue. (Don't look for a button labeled "ANY KEY", it won't be there, just pick a key and hit it!) MEMAKER's options are navigable using only three keys:

- Spacebar—toggle menu items
- F3—abort
- Enter—proceed with selection

When asked for Express or Custom setup, choose Custom. The next question asks if you need EMS or not. Unless you specifically know that you need EMS, say NO.

The next screen lists six questions. We'll take each one in turn.

- Specify drivers and TSRs - Answering YES to this question allows you to select the drivers and TSRs you do not want placed into upper memory (UMBs). Answer NO to this question, unless you're sure you need to exclude something from upper memory.

- Aggressive Scan—Answering YES to this option includes the memory area F000-F7FF which is otherwise excluded. If you encounter errors while running MEMMAKER or have trouble with your system, re-run MEMMAKER with this option set to NO.

- Optimize for Windows—Say NO, or say YES only if you NEVER run DOS based programs under Windows.

- Use monochrome region—Answer NO to this if you are using a monochrome or SuperVGA monitor, otherwise YES will include an area of memory usually reserved for these types of monitors.

- Keep current inclusions and exclusions—If you

have to exclude or include special areas of memory for hardware or software on your system, and you've already added these regions to the EMM386 line in your CONFIG.SYS file answer NO, otherwise YES will give MEMMAKER complete freedom to change these regions.

- Move extended BIOS data—Saying YES to this moves the extended BIOS data into upper memory. If you experience problems, say NO.

If MEMMAKER makes changes to your system that you don't like or that cause your system to function poorly, you can undo these changes by typing the following command at the DOS prompt:

```
MEMMAKER /UNDO
```

It's nice to know there's always a way back to where you started from, no matter how deep down the path to trouble and tribulation you might get!

SUMMARY

In this chapter, you've plumbed the depths of DOS memory management (or, at least as far as we can send you without a personal guide). There's plenty more unexplored territory to investigate beyond the areas we've covered, but you'll probably not have to venture into them unless curiosity propels you further into the great unknown. If you do venture forth into this uncharted territory, be sure to get a copy of John Goodman's *PC Memory Management* book, or an equivalent reference, to help you out along the way.

Video—Can You See the Light?

5

In this chapter, we'll discuss problems and difficulties you may encounter with video cards and monitors, and with programs that use video.

First reseat all connections and power cables. Then, reset your monitor and computer.

One common video problem occurs when you forget to exclude the video BIOS addresses from your memory manager under DOS and/or Windows. Many video cards use a BIOS address range of C000-C7FF (you'll need to check your video card's manual for the addresses for your particular card). This range of memory needs to be excluded from general memory usage, and this needs to occur in two files:

1. DOS: CONFIG.SYS. Using a text editor, locate the memory manager line. If you are using DOS 5.0 or higher, and no third party memory managers, the file name will be EMM386.SYS. At the end of this line, add **X=C000-C7FF**. This excludes that memory block from being used (except by your video card). Be sure only

to exclude the correct memory addresses, and that you use the proper syntax and parameters for your particular memory manager.

2. Windows: SYSTEM.INI. Using a text editor, locate the section that begins with **[386Enh]**. Immediately under this line, add **EMMExclude=C000-C7FF**. This will exclude the memory area from Windows' use.

Use bundled diagnostic and installation (e.g., MSD.EXE or the video card's own) utilities to verify that the settings on your card match the settings in the software.

Be sure that you have selected the correct monitor type during installation. Many high-end video cards can modify their signals to match the requirements for different monitors.

 Warning: If you have a monitor attached to your system that differs from the one you selected during your video card's set-up, you can possibly damage your monitor, depending on the nature of the resulting mismatch.

Double-check your installation to be sure that you've placed all of the proper drivers in the correct areas. Some cards require one driver for DOS and a second one for Windows. There are even cards that require separate drivers for different Windows applications!

Another possible problem area can arise from hardware configuration conflicts. Check the configuration settings for your video card against all the other expansion boards in your computer. Be sure that no two cards have overlapping addresses, IRQ, DMA settings, or other conflicting assignments.

Q2: What can I do about poor picture quality?

- Re-seat all connections and power cables. Reset your monitor and computer.

- Clean your monitor's glass surface with a glass cleaner and a soft cloth.

- Re-seat the video card in its bus connector. Alternatively, try changing its bus slot assignment. Before re-seating the card, use compressed air to remove dust from the bus connector.

- Magnetic interference can reduce picture quality. This occurs when a video cable is located near metal or a strong power source. Such interference can be countered by placing special rings, called ferrite cores, around each end of the cable, one near the card and another near the monitor (these rings are available at most computer stores).

  If your video cable has already been treated with ferrite rings, try rearranging your computer's layout to reroute your video cable. Keep it as far away from speakers, power supplies, or other devices as you can.

- Consult your manual about proper settings for your monitor—these include: contrast, brightness, geometry, color, etc.

- Change your display's resolution. Most software packages are designed for a 640 x 480 pixel screen (standard VGA). If you're using 800 x 600, 1024 x 768, or 1280 x 1024, try reducing the pixel dimensions and see if that helps.

- Change your display's color depth. Most software packages are designed for 256-color displays. If you're using 32K, 64K, or 16.7 million colors, reduce the color depth and try the software again.

Q3: I just installed new software, and now Windows won't work. What can I do?

Many software packages change your Windows video setup by adding new drivers or changing video modes. Too often the installation process does not inform you about the changes it makes—look in the software's manual for those changes. The new software may be user-friendly enough to create backup copies of those files it changed, or it may not be. But to get back to work, you're going to have to restore your system to its prior condition.

In order to restore your system, try the following operations:

- Exit to DOS and run the Windows Setup utility. Restore the video driver back to its previous setting (prior to the software's installation). Usually, this would be VGA or some driver supplied with your video card (you should have this information in your CIF).

- Next, try to restore those files that the installation changed, using your backup copies.

- Using the manual, edit out or remove all the changes made to your system configuration.

Note: *resetting the video mode may cause the new software to stop working. You may need to reinstall the software, and select an option that lets you use your current video mode or driver. If this doesn't appear to be a valid option, call the software vendor's technical support line for help.*

Q4: The software runs, but my videos skip, stutter, pause or have jerky sound. How can I fix this?

If the software functions properly, except for video portions, this usually indicates that your system isn't fast or powerful enough to play all the video frames at the same speed as the audio. The video driver is probably dropping frames to keep pace with the sound, or it may be playing all the video frames, thereby causing the sound to break up. Possible remedies for this include:

- Some DOS packages that offer options to vary the parameters for video and audio playback. Consult your software manual to locate the option menu. Try one of the following options, if available:
  - Reduce the number of frames per second displayed.
  - Select "skip frames if behind."
  - Reduce the number of audio voices.
  - Turn off either FX, voice or music sound.
  - Decrease the size of the video window.
  - Reduce the color depth.

- Allow transfer of the video segment to hard disk before playback (this is faster than reading from your CD-ROM, but can require significant amounts of available disk space).

- Increase or decrease the RAM used for the video cache.

- Keep a log of your attempts to fix the problems, and note the results. Restore settings to original values when changes don't help, or don't make a noticeable difference.

- Add or remove the CD-ROM cache utility. Experiment with the settings available. The player's manual, or the utility's read.me files, should suggest applicable settings. Here again, keep a log and stick only with settings that help, rather than hinder your CD's operation (or which leave it apparently unchanged).

- Update your video driver. You may need to search CompuServe, the Internet or call the video card vendor's Tech Support to locate new drivers for your card.

 Watch Out! Be sure to install only those new drivers specifically designed for your make, model and brand of video card; you can damage your card and/or your monitor if you use the wrong ones.

- Under Windows, change playback options in the Drivers application in Control Panel. Some video drivers have settings to vary the playback method. For example, Video for Windows gives you the options: of **zoom, full screen, window,** and most importantly **skip frames if behind** (as shown in Figure 5-1.) Use the one that gets

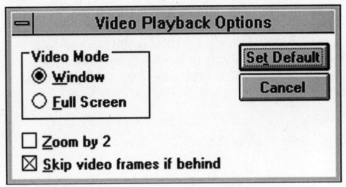

Figure 5.1: The Video for Windows playback options.

you the best results.

- You may have an outdated Windows video player. If you haven't updated your Windows QuickTime or Video for Windows software in the past three months, there's probably a newer version available. The software that requires one of these players will include the latest version, usually on the same CD. You can also find these on CompuServe or the Internet. Be careful only to install a newer version; don't replace a newer version with an older one, or you may make things worse instead of better!

- Consider upgrading your video card's on-board memory. There are two types of video memory: DRAM and VRAM. **DRAM,** or dynamic RAM, is slow because it needs to constantly refresh the information it stores, and because it's unable to be read from and written to at the same time.

  VRAM, or video RAM, is faster because it can be read from and written to simultaneously. Unfortunately, VRAM costs two to five times as much as DRAM.

69

Most software packages recommend video cards with at least 1MB of on-board RAM (usually they mean VRAM, rather than DRAM). Upgrading to a 2M VRAM video card can greatly increase the quality of images displayed on your monitor, and the speeds at which they can be displayed.

Q5: What is the VESA BIOS Extension?

The VESA BIOS Extension is a set of standards from the Video Electronics Standards Association. These standards allow a software package to interact with a large range of SVGA cards without requiring a separate driver for each one.

Most SVGA cards today support the common VESA interface. Some cards require a video system call to activate the VESA BIOS stored on a separate video chip. In any case, your video card's manual should explain how it complies with the VESA standards.

If you encounter difficulty running a software package that requires VESA, after reading your manual, you may need to call the software vendor's tech support, then possibly the video card vendor's tech support. Your system may require a driver update, or you may have a non-VESA compliant card. The update will be easy to come by and should put you back to work as soon as it's installed; a lack of VESA compliance leaves you only two choices: bag the software, or buy a new video card.

Q6: I purchased a 17" monitor (or larger), but when I run some software the pictures are jagged and I can see individual pixels. Shouldn't a large monitor behave better than this?

Larger monitors give you more pixels per inch, and allow you to have more graphical information on-screen than a 14" monitor. However, increased size and display capabilities are only useful for programs that can change video display modes.

Most graphical games and CD-ROM based video programs do not have the ability to change video modes. On a larger monitor, a 640x480 display mode will be stretched across a larger surface area. This reduces clarity and increases the relative size of the pixels. Your only options, alas, are to (a) live with it, or (b) get a second smaller monitor just for these programs.

SUMMARY

In this chapter, we've looked at the most common ways that video and display issues can cloud your enjoyment of your CD-ROM's software-handling capabilities. By far, the most common source of video problems is loose connections, so be sure to check those first. On the other hand, you'll have to become more expert in updating drivers and choosing display modes if you want to get the best out of your system under all circumstances. Since seeing really is believing, we hope you'll be seeing what you like from your system real soon now!

Keyboards, Joysticks, and Mouses: Should We Get More Cheese?

6

In this chapter, we'll discuss some of the problems and difficulties you're likely to encounter with keyboards, joysticks and mice. (Some of the CompuServe Sysops on the Microsoft forums insist that mice is only a valid plural for the small furry rodents, and that the plural of the computer pointing device called a mouse should be "mouses." We don't think so, but it makes for a catchy Chapter title, don't you think?)

Q1: My keyboard doesn't work, or a few keys no longer function. What can I do?

If your keyboard fails to operate properly, there are only three possible culprits.

1. The connection between the keyboard and the computer may be loose or dusty, or the key-

board cable that connects the two may be
damaged or broken.

2. The keyboard's electronics may be damaged.

3. Your computer's motherboard may be damaged.

The first problem can be diagnosed quickly with
a little compressed air and a quick reconnect. Be sure
to reboot before you try your connection again. If all
else fails, borrow an identical keyboard cable from
someone and see if this fixes the problem; if it does,
you're going to need to buy a new one.

The second and third problems are more sub-
stantial. Before you throw anything away, try a second keyboard and try the 'defective' keyboard on a
different computer. A broken keyboard is useless—
mark it for delivery to the sanitation department,
then visit your local computer retailer. A bad motherboard is bad news, so if you suspect your motherboard is having problems, take your system to a
computer repair center.

Q2: My joystick is not functioning or doesn't per-form like it should. What can I do?

Every single device or part of a computer has a
driver, and the joystick is no exception. Generally a
software package that requires a joystick includes a
game port or joystick port driver. But there are many
types of joystick interfaces that you might have on
your system. You'll need to find out what type you
have before you can troubleshoot your problem.

- Sound cards, especially Sound Blaster models,

may have joystick ports. These may be turned on or off using jumpers on the sound card. Sometimes the default is "on" but other times it's "off," so you'll need to consult the sound card's manual to verify that the port is enabled.

- I/O cards that control your floppy drives (FD), hard drives (HD), serial ports and parallel ports may also include a game port. Like the sound card, the port must be enabled in order to use it. Once again, you'll have to haul out a manual and figure out if the game port is turned on or not.

- Sometimes, computers even include special-purpose game card adapters. Some joysticks come with interface cards designed specifically for them. Game cards are also available by themselves. Usually, a game card requires a special driver to be loaded to make it compatible with other software packages. A game card/joystick combination may give you specialty options including sensitivity, response delay, auto-fire, extra button definitions, pedals, and even headset attachments. If you (or another member of your family) is a serious gamer, you may want to look into buying one of these (even with a super-duper joystick, you'll seldom pay more than $150 for such a package).

- Motherboards also include built-in game port adapters these days. Although they're uncommon, these types of systems support joysticks directly, without requiring yet another expansion card.

If your joystick or game port requires a special driver, your manual should state this clearly. If not, your port and joystick should be fully compatible with any software package that supports a joystick.

When your joystick fails to work:

- Check the connection. Use compressed air to remove dust.

- Check the joystick's physical calibration. Many joysticks have calibration wheels in their bases. Usually the center (or "sweet spot") for these wheels is marked. Reposition these markings to the top center.

- Most software packages have a joystick calibration routine; use it to recalibrate your joystick. Be careful to follow the on-screen directions and to press your fire button only once per setting.

- Some joysticks have PC/MAC compatability switches on their bases. Make sure the selection matches your system.

- Some joysticks have auto-fire capabilities. Some software programs are incompatible with the signals this option produces. Generally, start a game with the auto-fire off and only switch it on if the game doesn't offer software auto-fire.

- Check to see if you should be using a driver that should be loaded in AUTOEXEC.BAT or CONFIG.SYS for your port adapter or joystick model.

- Use a different joystick, and use your joystick on a different machine; yours may be damaged. This quick test will let you know right away.

- Some software packages use the joystick, keyboard and mouse interchangeably. Other packages use only one at a time. When one of your input devices doesn't work, try using another one. Many games switch between joystick flight control, mouse menu control and keyboard movement control without informing you that the control device has changed. A little experimentation will help you figure out if this is the case.

- Some software packages have a configuration utility to select and configure the input device. Check to see that the correct settings and device types are saved.

- Re-seat your port adapter in a different bus slot.

If you have tried all these, you should call the software tech support. Most likely an undocumented switch, bug, patch or driver is required.

Q3: Eek! Why won't my mouse work?

The mouse is a quiet sensitive beast that requires care and feeding. Mainly it needs to be clean, securely leashed, and fed the proper driver.

- Check the mouse cord, and be sure the connection to the serial port is secure and free of dust.

- Check to see that the driver loads properly.

  - Under DOS, locate the driver file (it will be called something like mouse.com; check your mouse manual). If the driver can be loaded from a command prompt, enter the file name and the driver will report that it found a mouse and is loaded. You may need to consult the mouse's manual to determine the proper method for loading the driver.

- For Windows, you'll need to run the setup utility (SETUP.EXE) from DOS; this program is usually located in the main Windows directory. Be sure the input device reads Microsoft mouse or the type of mouse you own. You may be prompted to insert one of the Windows install diskettes. After setup has been completed, you'll need to start Windows to see if the mouse works or not.

- If you're not using a bus mouse (which needs no COM port), try switching the COM port your mouse is plugged into. You should have at least 2 COM ports available on your computer. Usually com1 is a 9-pin D connector and com2 is a 25-pin D connector, so you may require a 9-to-25 pin converter to switch ports. Some mouse drivers will only function on one port or the other, while others must be informed the port where the mouse is attached. The instructions for the driver should explain its parameters and operation.

- You may need to update your mouse driver. New mouse drivers are available on CompuServe and the Internet. Look for information in an area where the Mouse vendor provides information (e.g. GO MSMOUSE on CompuServe, and on ftp.microsoft.com on the Internet).

- You might have a dirty mouse. On most mice, you can remove the rolling ball. This should be cleaned with warm water and mild soap. Thoroughly dry the ball before replacing it. If you are handy with a screw driver, you can open the mouse and dust it out with compressed air. You can also readjust the sensors on either side of the spinning wheels. CAUTION! These photo cells are fragile and can be broken easily; make only minor adjustments, if any. They should be less than 1/8th inch from the wheel and each pair should be parallel to the other.

- Try another mouse on your computer and try your mouse on a different computer.

- Be cautious of mice that claim 100% compatibility. Of all computer hardware, mice are usually the best at being compatible, but there are still some that don't measure up. If a mouse doesn't specifically state in its documentation that it's Microsoft Mouse compatible, don't use it!

If your mouse still doesn't operate, you may need to give it to the cat and go get yourself a replacement. For our money, we still like the genuine Microsoft Mouse the best!

SUMMARY

In this chapter we've looked at the things that can go wrong with your input devices—specifically your keyboard, mouse, and joystick—that might interfere with your ability to enjoy the concentrated firepower and adroit maneuvering required to get the most out of your CD-ROM and its many great games!

Modems—Can You Make the Call?

7

In this chapter, we will discuss problems and difficulties that you might encounter when using a modem with your CD-ROM player (probably for one of the newer, multiuser, interactive games like WarCraft: Orcs and Humans).

> **Q1: My new software program cannot locate my modem, or it fails to operate the modem. What can I do?**

Most setup utilities on new software programs will ask you for the make, model and location of your modem. You should have all this information listed in your CIF. However, installation of those slick modem programs is not foolproof.

Let's do a little snooping to eliminate a few suspects—as Sherlock Holmes stated "Once you've eliminated the impossible, whatever is left, however improbable, must be the truth."

- Reboot your entire system and recheck the new software.

- Check to see if the modem still functions with other terminal emulation or communications programs you used prior to the new software's installation. This will help you to determine if the new program has altered your system. If your system has been changed, you may need to uninstall the new software to get your modem working again. Take some time to review the installation instructions and, if necessary, call the new software company's technical support for help.

- Check to see if the modem's power is turned on.

- Make sure you have a proper modem cable (tx–rx). You can look at the signals using the Microsoft Diagnostics program (MSD.EXE).

- Double-check the modem's configuration and location.

- Run the Setup or configuration utility for the new program to verify that the proper modem settings were entered (and saved).

- If your modem is external, dust and re-seat all connections. Reset or re-power the modem. If it's an internal model, dust the modem's bus slot and connector pins. Consider seating the card in a different bus slot if re-seating doesn't do the trick.

- Browse the software manual for compatible modem and emulation types. If yours is not listed, try a similar modem type or use the Hayes default. (If you do not have a Hayes-compatible modem, consider purchasing one.)

- Check your modem's manuals for its emulation modes and how to operate them.

- Check the modem command strings used by the software to operate your modem. You can use the command strings from another functioning program or consult your modem's manual for its charts of valid command strings.

- Check for comm port conflict. There are generally 4 COM port definitions available for use by software and hardware. Most I/O cards have 2 COM ports that can be configured for any of the 4 possible definitions. The standard IRQ settings for comm ports are as follows:

IRQ	COM Port Ids
IRQ 3	COM2 & COM4
IRQ 4	COM1 & COM3

No two comm ports on the same IRQ can operate at the same time. You will need to check that your modem and mouse [or other device] are on separate IRQs.

- Try switching the modem's COM port. You will need to reboot the computer and reconfigure for the modem's new location. A few of the play-by-modem CD-ROM based games we tested required the modem to be on COM1, contrary to the software's manual. Always try other possible settings when a configuration fails, but generally, the default configuration is the most reliable (unfortunately, using defaults isn't always possible).

  - For external modems simply attach the connector to another serial port. You may need a 9-to-25 pin D converter to do this.

  - For internal modems, you'll need to consult the manual for the settings required to change the COM port.

- Consult your modem's installation manual to verify that you have properly installed, configured, and set up the modem. Check the type of UART chip servicing your COM port; then check your speed settings (only 16550A or higher models can handle speeds in excess of 38.4 Kbps).

- Some modems, especially internal fax/modems require a driver. Be sure the driver is loaded from the proper startup file and has the correct parameters.

Q2: I just faxed a document successfully, so why won't my terminal program dial?

Fax/modems are quickly becoming the standard communications tool for home computers. Learning how to get the most out of one is sometime a little difficult. A Fax/modem is actually two devices in a single package—namely, a fax machine and a modem.

Any terminal program should be able to access the modem side of the device, but fax software usually needs to load special drivers to alter the modem's functions to enable the fax components in the device. Once those fax drivers are loaded into memory, a long command string is sent to the device to prepare it for sending or receiving documents. Even after you've exited the fax software, those fax drivers may remain active, so your modem will remain in fax mode.

Unfortunately, the fax mode is incompatible with standard modem terminal programs. The signals that faxes and modems use to transfer data are significantly different (although to your ear both carrier signals are annoying and high-pitched).

After using your fax software, here's what you'll need to do in order to use your terminal program again:

1. Reset your modem
   - External models—simply hit the reset button or re-power the device
   - Internal models require that you reboot your system.

2. Load and test your terminal program
   - If it works, connect and go about your business
   - If it doesn't work, this means the fax drivers were left in memory and you will need to reboot your system in order to remove them.

Q3: Why won't my machine's modem connect to another modem?

First, have both ends run through the solutions suggested in Q1 (if at all possible). After these potential fixes have been exhausted, you still have a few more approaches to try:

- Check all cables, including the phone line. Be sure the phone line is plugged into the connector that is labeled "wall" or "line". Verify that the wall jack functions (get a handset and see if you get a dial tone).

- Check the phone number you're dialing. You can even use your standard handset to dial the number and listen for a high pitched squeal to verify there's a modem on the other side of the connection.

- Be sure your modem is set to dial out and the other modem is set to auto-answer, or vice versa.

- Check the baud rate. The baud rate is the speed at which a modem can transmit and receive data. The commonly available baud rates are: 1200, 2400, 9600, 14400, and 28800. (If you are wondering why 300 is not listed, go back and play with your Commodore 64.) You will not only need to know your modem's maximum baud rate, but also that for the answering modem. You will only be able to operate at the lower of these two rates, so be sure your software is configured appropriately. Also, using an older UART chip with a high-speed modem can produce erroneous results, so be sure to match speeds with capabilities.

- Modern modems use communications protocols that take advantage of on-the-fly compression technology—in other words, these modems go faster. However, compression is not useful in every situation; sometimes, you may need to turn off compression, via a command string or a baud selection menu.

 Note: 19200, 38400, 57600 and 115200 are compression-based rates associated with 14400 or faster modems. These numbers do not represent the actual amount of data transmitted, but rather the projected amount based on a 1.33:1 to 8:1 possible compression

ratio. Higher compression occurs in data with high levels of repetition or regularity, while lower compression occurs in data with a low level of regularity or redundancy.

- In the U.S., phone line quality is slowly beginning to meet the requirements for high-speed data transmission. Even so, most modems communicate over older twisted-pair copper lines. Many of these analog lines have static problems because of their age, their composition, and their lack of insulation. If your initial try doesn't succeed, try again at least two or three times; you may have gotten a noisy line. In some areas, even a light storm can cause enough interference to prevent data transmission, especially in older neighborhoods with above-ground telephone lines.

SUMMARY

Although the intersection of CD-ROMs and modems is mostly tangential, some communications programs (like those for on-line access, e.g., CompuServe's WinCIM or MacCIM) and even some games require you to use both devices together. When this happens, you can get the best of both worlds if you make sure that each element is working properly. In this chapter, we've tried to clue you in to some of the common problems and gotchas that can prevent a successful CD-ROM communications experience.

ARRGGHH! Windows Broke, AGAIN!

8

In this chapter, we'll take a look at our favorite form of masochism—namely, MS Windows and its many foibles.

Q1: I installed a new program; now, Windows won't work. What can I do?

The first thing is to restore your system from the backups you made before installing your new software. What? You didn't make backups? Don't worry, all is not necessarily lost. You may still be able to restore your system. To learn your fate, please work through the following list of corrective procedures.

- First, reboot to make sure Windows is really hosed and it's not just a memory problem.

- Next, use the software's uninstall utility, if it has one, to reverse the changes it made to your system.

If these approaches fail, you're stuck. You'll have to restore your system manually (don't worry, after one or two rounds of this activity, you'll learn the value of backing up).

- Get to a DOS prompt (where else could you go?)

- Look in the windows directory for old copies of WIN.INI and SYSTEM.INI. Remember, if the software was kind enough to make backups of these files, the extensions will be changed. Look for the most recent copies in order to lose as little configuration information as possible. To look for these older versions try the following DOS commands:

```
CD \WINDOWS
DIR WIN.*
DIR SYSTEM.*
```

- If you're able to locate backups of these files, you're off to a good start. Before you put them back in place, make backups of the current "broken" files. You might discover that they aren't as broken as you thought. Something else may be amiss, so you may very well want these originals back. Create your own "special" backup file extension, .YUK, with the following DOS commands:

```
COPY WIN.INI WIN.YUK
COPY SYSTEM.INI SYSTEM.YUK
```

- Using the latest backup you could find, restore WIN.INI and SYSTEM.INI to their original names and locations (usually, this will be in the root Windows directory, e.g., C:). Assuming the backup WIN.INI is named WIN.BAK and the backup SYSTEM.INI is named, SYSTEM.OLD, the following DOS commands will begin this process

```
COPY WIN.BAK WIN.INI
COPY SYSTEM.OLD SYSTEM.INI
```

- After you've restored the files into their proper name places, reboot and test Windows.

- If this allows you to run Windows, your work may still be only partially complete. If you've restored a backup that was created just before the new software changed your system, everything should be back to your version of normalcy. But if you've restored a backup from days or weeks ago, you're probably now missing other configuration changes made during the interim. You have two choices to figure out what's missing.

  1. Run each and every one of the programs you've installed on your system to insure it functions correctly. If you discover any problems, you'll need either to reconfigure that program or reinstall it (try reconfiguring first; if that doesn't work, you'll have to reinstall, sorry).

  2. Compare the current versions of the INI files to those you copied with extension .YUK. The .YUK files will be closest to the preinstallation settings that you want restored. You can use two Notepad windows to compare them, or you can run a special application that compares files (such as WDiff–wdiff130.zip), or print out one of the files, and compare the printed one to the one on the screen. Working with one change at a time, add or remove information to the in-use INI files, based on what you see. Sure, it's laborious, time-consuming and not terribly reward-

ing, but this will help you to remember to backup next time!

- If restoring the INI backups doesn't fix Windows, the INI files may not be at fault. Run the Windows SETUP.EXE program from DOS (Hint: it's located in the main Windows subdirectory, e.g., C:). Be sure all of its settings listed match your system's configuration; even the slightest divergence can create major system snafus.

  - Check the video driver; if you don't recognize what's listed, switch back to VGA or to the correct driver for your video card.

  - If you're using a network, make sure the right network type is selected (and version, if applicable).

- Other problems may lurk in your CONFIG.SYS and AUTOEXEC.BAT files. Restore these files from backups if these have changed. If you don't have backups, open each in a text editor and look for changes. Without backups you'll have to guess, unless the software documents changes it makes to your system (we call this "well-behaved software, and we like this idea very much).

- If Windows remains broken, you have little choice but to reinstall Windows. Sometimes reinstalling can restore many of your settings, but at the very least it should provide you with a working Windows environment.

Q2: Windows runs but my screen is incorrectly sized, or the color depth or resolution has changed. How can I fix this?

It is all too common for new software to replace your video drivers, or to alter their setup during installation. To correct this problem you'll need to restore the correct video driver using the Windows Setup program. From Windows' Program Manager, select File Run and enter SETUP, or from DOS, run SETUP.EXE from the Windows subdirectory. Select the correct driver for your video card or VGA.

If restoring the driver doesn't correct the problem, the software may have changed the video driver's setup instead. You'll need to consult your video card's documentation to restore it to its previous settings.

If this restores your system, check to see that the new software still functions. If the software won't work, you will need to call tech support for a compromise solution that won't significantly alter your video driver, but will allow the new software to work, too.

Note: Some software packages will only work using a 256 color depth. If so, you'll need to keep your color depth set at 256 at all times, or you'll have to switch back and forth as you use the software with the more restrictive and less restrictive settings.

Q3: I just installed a software package; why won't my mouse work now?

Welcome to the world of driver roulette! The new software may have moved, deleted or changed your mouse driver. If your mouse doesn't work, check out Q3 in Chapter 6.

Q4: While using a new software package, Windows has started acting strangely. Fonts change sizes, letters disappear, icons black out, applications won't load, etc. What can I do?

These types of weirdness occur when the area of memory Windows has designated to store visual/graphical information has become full or corrupted (i.e. more than one device or program is trying to write to and read from the same memory locations).

If you can, try to exit and save your work, then reboot your computer. If you encounter this problem often, you may not have enough memory on your computer to support your customary level of work. Otherwise, you may have a poorly designed or malfunctioning memory manager, or you might have a latent driver conflict. To debug this kind of situation, you may find yourself working through Chapter 4 (Memory management), or you might try snooping for a naughty driver.

In cases like these, the process of elimination is often the only way to catch and correct the offending elements. If you've added hardware to your system, remove the new element and try the system without it. If the problems persist, they're probably software or driver related. If they desist, you've determined that something about the hardware settings are conflicting with other aspects of the system (which could be either hardware or software related).

Either way, you'll need to strip your system down to a bare minimum configuration (what Microsoft calls a "clean boot"). This means your CONFIG.SYS and AUTOEXEC.BAT files should include only the memory manager and the device drivers you absolutely must have to test the problem software (e.g., it's hard to test a CD-ROM based program without loading the SCSI or IDE driver for the drive, the CD-ROM extensions, and the multimedia drivers needed for sound, etc.).

Then, you can add elements to this clean boot, by themselves, one at a time, and look for problems. If this doesn't work, start adding them two at a time, then three at a time, until the problem recurs. Whatever you've added to your configuration most recently is the most likely culprit for the problem. Then, you can call the problem element's vendor's technical support hot line to try to figure what to do next. Although a formal process of elimination takes planning—and time, lots of time—it's sometimes the only way to catch and fix the kinds of elusive problems that the interaction among numerous drivers and system elements can cause.

SUMMARY

In this chapter, we've visited the tip of a pretty formidable iceberg—namely, MS Windows in its many varieties and guises. Windows is indeed a whole world unto itself, so if what we've exposed here doesn't provide you the depth of trouble-shooting information you need, we strongly recommend obtaining a catch-all Windows reference, like Brian Livingston's **Windows Secrets, More Windows Secrets,** or his newly-minted **Windows 95 Secrets** (depending, of course, on what version of Windows you're running; all of these books are published by IDG Books Worldwide, Indianapolis, IN, Copyrights 1993, 1994, and 1995, respectively). Any of these books should prove quite helpful in taking the next step down the tortuous trail to Windows Nirvana!

You Mean, I Need Other Software Too!?

9

In this chapter, we'll discuss some software and utilities that can be useful, but aren't absolutely mandatory to get the most out of your CD-ROM, and the CDs you purchase. Nevertheless, we think you'll find enough value here to be worth your time (and maybe, some of your money).

Q1: What software do I need to operate my CD-ROM at its best?

- The most important software you'll need for your CD-ROM is the driver and its installation utility. Periodically, you may want to search CompuServe or the Internet for updates to your drivers.

- Next, you'll need the Microsoft CD-ROM Extensions (MSCDEX.EXE) provided with DOS, preferably from DOS 6.2 or better. MSCDEX allows your CD-ROM drive to operate like a standard disk drive and assigns it a logical drive number. MSCDEX must be loaded after the CD-ROM's driver is loaded. While there are several third party CD-ROM Extension drivers, Helix's Multimedia Cloaking is a reliable product we have used ourselves. You'll need to consult the users manual for installation options that are applicable to your system's configuration.

- You'll want a disk cache to increase performance for most CD-ROMs. DOS is bundled with Smart-Drive, but only version 6.2 or higher can cache a CD-ROM. Most third-party caching utilities work like SmartDrive, although they may add functions and/or require less memory. You'll need to search the market to find which implementation works best for you. Then, you'll need to consult the users manual for installation options that are applicable to your system's configuration.

- A memory manager is highly recommended, sometimes mandatory—namely, for Windows Enhanced Mode operation. DOS's EMM386 is a good memory manager to use with a CD-ROM drive and Windows, but we have also had great experiences with QEMM386 (especially, versions 7.1 and 7.5). You'll need to consult your memory manager's users manual for installation options applicable to your system's configuration.

- Don't forget to investigate the software that ships with your system's components. This includes your CD-ROM, many of which ship with bundled audio players, sound editing programs, and more. This is an obvious avenue for investigation, but one worth trying nonetheless. Other less obvious avenues may be provided by the CD-ROM's adapter card (especially if you're using a name-brand SCSI adapter like an Adaptec or a PPI, both of which ship with several megabyte's worth of software and utilities), and by your sound card's vendor (much of the same stuff you'll get with a SCSI card, except more elaborate sound handling and editing software is typically included).

- Some third-party companies offer abundant CD-ROM utilities as standalone products—most notably, Corel Corporation's Corel SCSI software. This bundle of goodies includes a variety of viewers, players, and sound-editing tools, along with drivers for nearly every CD-ROM player known to man.

Q2: What software do I need to view movies and graphics?

The software you need is determined by the file type that you want to view. Most movie players can only display one type of movie. Some of the most common movie formats and viewers include the following:

- Apple QuickTime—these files take the extension .mov. Developed for use on Apple MAC computers, there is now a standard port process to 'flatten' the videos for use on PCs. These movies are most often viewed under Windows with the QuickTime for Windows drivers and player named player.exe. On CompuServe, GO QTW and follow the instructions (it will cost $10 for the download); on the Internet, point your Web browser at http://www.fagg.uni-lj.si/SHASE/ (here again, use QuickTime as a keyword).

- Video for Windows—these files take the extension .avi. To view these you will need the latest release of Video for Windows. On CompuServe, GO DTPFORUM (Desktop Publishing Forum) and check the PC DTP Utility library; on the Internet, point your Web browser at http://www.acs.oakland.edu/cgi-bin/shase (here again, use Video for Windows as a keyword).

- MPEG movies take the extension .mpg. These require an mpeg player. There are many shareware and freeware versions of mpeg players, however most are crippled to play only mpegs of less than 1M. One release which will play both mpeg-1 and mpeg-2 files of any length is the MPEG Software Simulation Group's Mpeg-2 Video Decoder. This file is available in the Internet for FTP, its compressed file name is MPG2W11B.ZIP. On CompuServe, GO PCFF to enter the PC File Finder, then use the compressed file name to locate the MPEG player file.

Q3: How can I view the graphics on a CD-ROM disc?

Most graphics discs include viewers, but if you want to explore on your own, you might try one of these graphics viewers:

- Paint Shop Pro (PSP) 3.0-A snappy graphics viewer/editor that displays 35 different graphics file formats, including: .jpg, .gif, .pcx, .tif and .bmp. PSP offers you a number of drawing tools, graphic filters, color palette editors and conversion options. The latest version at our disposal on the Internet has a file name of PSP30.ZIP.

- Lview Pro—A wonderfully fast .JPG viewer with loads of options. Lview can display over a dozen file formats, offers quite a few editing tools, most notable is creating transparent .gifs. The latest version at our disposal on the Internet has a file name of LVIEWP19.ZIP.

- VuePrint—Is a great slide show program to browse through numerous graphics. VuePrint has the ability to view not only graphics but sounds, movies and a few other file types. VuePrint offers a few editing options, but it has numerous display parameters and slide show options to capture your attention. The latest version at our disposal on the Internet has a file name of VUPRNT40.ZIP.

Q4: How can I listen to sounds from a CD-ROM?

If the sound files have the file extensions: .wav or .mid, this is easily accomplished with the Windows media player or an audio application bundled with your sound card. If you want another option, there is a good, temporary-use, sound editor available on the Internet called GoldWave. Its file is named GLD-WAV21.ZIP.

Q5: There are a bunch of files on my CD-ROM which I cannot get any third-party application to read or understand. Is something wrong?

Probably not. Many CD-ROM manufacturers use proprietary software programs to protect their work. Usually, they employ an in-house compression utility and decompress on-the-fly, or they'll create a new file format that's unreadable by standard applications.

If you can't read a file from a CD-ROM using a third party application; don't worry, all this means is that the software company has successfully blocked your curiosity from invading their copyrighted materials. Wherever possible, try to use the bundled software to view and operate a CD-ROM, that's why it's there, anyway.

SUMMARY

In this chapter, we've introduced you to a number of potential "helper" applications, that can make viewing or playing back the information on your CD-ROMs easier (and possibly, more fun). As you get more familiar with your equipment and your software, you'll find more reasons to use these tools to help you get the most enjoyment out of your CD-ROMs' software.

Look Out! 10
Some Software
Hurts More
Than It Helps!

In this chapter, we will briefly discuss some of the problems and difficulties you're likely to encounter when using poorly designed software packages and installation utilities. Fortunately, such encounters are infrequent (but not unknown). When they do occur, there's usually not much you can do about them, except to decide to put up with their behavior, or to bypass them altogether.

What we'd really like to see for software is a "truth in packaging" law that would require a warning label on software that included items like:

- **Warning!** This program will edit your AUTOEXEC.BAT and CONFIG.SYS files without warning, and without backing up the original versions.

- **Warning!** This program can only be installed in the C:directory; any attempts to relocate it will result in the end of computing as you know it!

- **Warning!** This program will cheerfully overwrite any earlier versions of this program, including any and all of the configuration information you've so laboriously created over the past few months (or years). Live with it!

If only this information were available, you'd be able to perform the most essential preinstallation activity of all: backing your system up. With such ill-behaved software ready to wreak havoc on your system, a backup is the only protection you have against such software malfeasance. Even though software doesn't include such warnings, we think you should go ahead and back things up anyway... If you're not convinced by now, we hope you will be by the end of this chapter!

> **Q1: The installation utility did not ask me for a target directory; instead, it added a directory and files to my C drive, but I wanted them only on the D drive. Why?**

Installation utilities that don't supply options to place the files they add to your system are worse than visits from your in-laws. As with the in-laws, there's little you can do about such ill-mannered installations.

There is one possible workaround, but it requires careful note-taking during the process. Also, this workaround may do the job of successfully relocating the program, so you'll need to undo the changes you make (hence the note-taking requirement). If the installation program creates a new directory on your C drive where most of its files reside, try the following relocation maneuvers:

- Move the directory to a new subdirectory or drive. This can be done from the DOS prompt, as follows:

```
CD C:\
XCOPY C:\ROBOTS\*.* D:\ROBOTS\ /S /E
```

- You should now have a duplicate directory on drive D. After you've built a backup, you can then delete the original directory (and any of its subdirectories) with this DOS command:

```
DELTREE C:\ROBOTS
```

- In the new directory, look for a file with configuration information or option settings. Normally, these files will include one of the following extensions in their names: .INI, .CFG or .DAT. Try to open the file using a text editor (EDIT or Notepad are fine). If you can, look for lines that include the original path and change them to reflect the new path.

- You might also need to edit the PATH statement (located in the AUTOEXEC.BAT file) to include mention of the software's new location. For example, you could add a reference to the new D:at the end of that statement, as follows:

```
PATH C:\;C:\DOS;D:\;C:\WINDOWS;D:\ROBOTS
```

- After rebooting, try to access the software from its new location. If it works, do a little happy dance. If not, delete the new directory and restore the original directory from your backup. You'll just have to live with the software in its default home.

Please note that this is only a suggestion; in many cases, this approach won't work. But if removing the software from your C:\ drive is absolutely non-negotiable, our suggestions comprise your only do-it-your-self option; otherwise, you'll have to call the manufacturer for a patch, fix or other workaround.

> **Q2: The installation utility didn't ask for permission to overwrite my previous configuration for an older version. Why not?**

Well, if the nasty little installation utility overwrote your previous configuration, you can always restore that configuration from your backups. Be sure you save the new versions, which you don't want, before restoring the old ones, which you do want.

Because the organization and format of the program's various configuration files can sometimes change between versions, the software may not function properly when new software combines with an old configuration. If this happens, you'll need to restore the new version and be forced to rebuild your configuration by hand, or you may elect to stick with the old version and not upgrade at all. If you don't have backups and the new software/old configuration combination doesn't work, you'll have to reset your configuration by hand. This time, make a backup. See Chapter 1 Q5.

> **Q3: The installation utility added commands to my startup files without asking. The installation utility did not make backups of the startup files it changed. The installation utility did not create a log of the changes it made to my system. Why do these things happen to me?**

In these days of peace and harmony on the desktop, start-up file violations still occur far too often. Unless you have previolation backups, you'll have to clean up your startup files manually. Without backups and/or change logs, knowing what to remove will be as easy for you as it would be for us, or a real pain in the you-know-what. See Chapter 1 Q6, Chapter 3 Q6, Chapter 5 Q3 and Chapter 8 for some strategies you can employ under these circumstances (after you've calmed down enough to want to solve the problem somebody else created for you).

Q4: The installation/setup utility doesn't provide an uninstall option. Why not?

Software can be a little rude at times. All too often, software lacks the same uninstall utility that your in-laws also lack. Removing software can be as easy as deleting a directory and an icon, to as hard as forcing you to reinstall DOS and Windows.

There are a few third-party uninstaller utilities that can aid you with this cleanup exercise, but these packages are most useful when they're also used to install the software in the first place. When used during installation, an uninstaller builds a log of all the changes, additions and edits that occur on your system. When the same utility is used to remove software, it then uses this log to restore your system to its original pristine condition. This is especially helpful in the Windows environment, where small subtle changes can sometimes have big, ugly consequences!

Even if you haven't used an uninstaller to monitor previous software installations, these programs' abilities to root around and remove unneeded drivers and hidden files may still be a great help. You might give one of these programs a try: MicroHelp's Uninstaller 2, IMSI's WinDelete and QuarterDeck's Clean Sweep. See Chapter 1 Q6, Chapter 3 Q6, Chapter 5 Q3 and Chapter 8 if you have to try uninstalling by hand.

Q5: The installation utility changed Windows' video mode, or some other operational driver, or my Windows INI files, or Windows no longer functions. Why did it do this to me?

Many installation utilities are as nice to Windows as a flying brick is comforting to a bay window. Restoring from backups, uninstalling or manual restoration/reconfiguration are your only options for recovering from such ill-mannered programs. Before you start down the road to reconstructing your system, please take the time to consult the other chapters in this book about those areas on your system that have been affected. Especially, see Chapter 1 Q6, Chapter 3 Q6, Chapter 5 Q3 and Chapter 8.

Q6: The installation utility added a group window under Program Manager without asking. The installation utility did not ask which group to add the new icons to. Why?

Sometimes, software installations will drop little presents all over your desktop, where you least want them. You can move them with a Windows drag-n-drop or select File, Move, and then select the target group. If a new group or icon shows up that you don't want hanging around, you can remove it. Be sure to move any useful icons to other groups first, and then minimize the offending group's window. Select the minimized group icon, then File Delete. Removing icons is as simple as selecting the icon, then File Delete, or hitting the Delete key on the keyboard. If you don't want 'em, you can make 'em leave!

Q7: The software requires me to reconfigure my sound/video/SCSI/etc. card back to the factory default, but all my other software and hardware works fine with the current configuration. What should I do?

Take a moment, scoot away from your desk, lean back and scream—"This is a completely unreasonable demand!" If you run across a software package with such requirements, contact the manufacturer directly and firmly request a fix, a patch, or your money back. If you actually want to accommodate this ridiculous request, block out at least 5 to 6 months to reconfigure all of your hardware and software. You'll also need to find new nonconflicting configurations for each product, then retest the offending software. Take a few moments to consult the rest of this book for a few hints, especially Chapter 1. Our advice is "Just Say No!"

Q8: The software did things that the documentation left out, or that it didn't explain completely. Why?

Frustration begins with stupidity—not yours—but rather, that of the creator of the lovely software that just imposed anarchy on your system. If you can determine what was done, do your best to undo these changes, and please take the time to consult the suggestions in each relevant chapter of this book.

If a solution eludes you after repeated efforts, restore your system from your backup. If you can't do this, give the offending program's tech support people a call, and tell them how unhappy you are in excruciating and complete detail.

SUMMARY

The answer to all of these questions shares a fundamental cause: poorly designed software. There is simply no excuse for software manufacturers to behave so inconsiderately during the installation and operation of their products. Every time you're faced with a manufacturer-designed defect or a poor installation utility, call or write the company. Be sure to talk with someone in management, public relations or software development.

You might even consider writing a letter to a magazine or to an on-line newsgroup. Before you make your voice heard, however, you do need to be absolutely sure of your facts. Here's how to cuss them out with confidence:

- Always call tech support to verify that the problem originates with the software and not with you (operator error is still the most common cause for computer conundrums). Also find out if there is a fix, a patch, an update, or a documentation addendum that addresses the issue. You may not be the first to encounter this problem, and there may even be a solution to this problem.

- Be sure the problem is repeatable. If it's only happened once, it's not a design flaw, its a "Murphy attack."

- Double-check the documentation. Be sure it doesn't address your problem, or confirm that it misinformed you about your problem.

- Try reinstalling to verify that options and choices you'd swear were missing aren't lurking somewhere that you failed to notice the first time around.

- Always include information about your system and any unique configurations you use.

If we consumers demand high-quality, user-friendly software, manufacturers will eventually capitulate. But this will require each of us to make the call, write the letter or send the e-mail that voices this demand, over and over again.

Speed and Optimization— How Fast Is Fast Enough?

11

In this chapter, we will give you some hints, tips and tricks for speeding up your current system. Sometimes, being able to make the most of what you've got is more than enough to get you where you need to go, without having to expend too much effort or money to get there!

Q1: How can I get my CD-ROM drive to work faster?

Despite the claims you'll occasionally hear from drive-caching software vendors, there's really no way to get your CD-ROM drive to work faster than its maximum throughput rate will allow. But you can help it to perform as designed. Likewise, you can also prepare your system to handle the information flow from your CD-ROM as quickly and efficiently as possible. Here's how:

- To begin with, please reread the CD-ROM solutions covered in Chapter 2.

- Get the latest driver updates for your CD-ROM drive and its interface card (whether SCSI or proprietary). These are often available on the Internet or CompuServe, although you may need to call the manufacturer to get information about where and how to retrieve these files.

- Use a disk cache that works with CD-ROM drives. The version of SmartDrive included with MS DOS 6.2 has this ability, for example, and there are numerous third-party disk caches that support CD-ROM drives as well (e.g., Future Systems Solutions' SpeedCache, Symantec's Norton Utilities NCACHE2, or PC-Kwik Corporation's Super PC-Kwik 6.0). Whatever disk cache you choose, experiment with buffer sizes for both DOS and Windows to determine the best settings for each environment.

- A disk cache may sometimes cause data transfer from your CD-ROM to be interrupted (it's a dead giveaway when your CD-ROM drive's activity light flashes off for seconds at a time in the middle of large data transfers, like launching an application or loading a large graphic, etc.). If you suspect this is happening, turn CD-ROM caching off. Using SmartDrive, for example, enter SMARTDRV.EXE /U in the AUTOEXEC.BAT; here, /U tells SMARTDRV not to cache the CD-ROM drive. Other disk caches typically offer similar capabilities, but will use their own special syntax; for the details, check their manuals or these programs' on-line help facilities (where applicable).

Q2: How can I improve my system's performance?

Usually, system performance is a function of memory use. If you have at least 8M of memory, you should be able to handle most software adequately (even then, some programs like CAD packages or high-resolution graphics software may require 16 or even 32M).

- Review the suggestions in Chapter 4 about moving modules to upper memory. Do whatever you can to free up your PC's conventional memory.

- Try to use Windows' 32 bit disk access and its 32 bit file access, if at all possible. These features are accessed through the Virtual Memory button in the 386 Enhanced application of the Control Panel. You may need to consult your hard drives' documentation to determine if they're compatible with this feature. If you experience any problems, turn off the disk access feature first. It's a common culprit for such unexpected side effects!

- Under Windows, create a virtual memory space around 8M in size (unless you have a program that specifically requests more). This feature may be set from the 386 Enhanced application in the Control Panel. From within this program, select Virtual Memory, then Change>>.

  Once you select the Change button, a series of selections will pop up in a subwindow labeled "New Settings." Here's what you'll need to do:

  1. Select your fastest hard drive (and make sure it's got sufficient space available; most Windows pundits recommend that you take the time to defragment your drive before setting up a permanent swap file because this will locate that file optimally on your drive)

2. Select the Permanent option in the Type entry field, and enter 8192 in the New Size field.

3. You'll need to restart Windows for these new settings to take effect.

- You might be loading a lot of programs that are not essential to every Windows session. Programs are loaded from two places, the StartUp group window and from the initial [windows] section in the WIN.INI file.

  - You can get to the StartUp group window from the Program Manager, Select Window from the menu bar, then # StartUp. (The # represents the number assigned to the listed windows.) If the StartUp name is not listed, select More Windows... to get a longer list. Any program in this group is loaded every time Windows starts up. If there are nonessential programs here, move them to another group. This is done by a drag-n-drop or select File, Move, then select the target group for the move.

  - To find out what's loaded in the WIN.INI file, use Notepad or some other text editor to edit that file (WIN.INI is in the main Windows sub-directory).

    There are two lines located near the beginning of this file. One starts with "load=" and the other "run=". Here's the skinny on these two statements:

    - Any file that appears within the "load=" statement will run minimized (i.e., with only an icon showing on the desktop).

    - Any file listed after the "run=" statement

will be loaded in a standard (maximized) window.

- You can either delete a file name or move it to a new line with a semi-colon ";" at the head to prevent it from loading. For example:

```
load=write.exe notepad.exe winword.exe
run=
```

can be changed to:

```
load=write.exe notepad.exe
;winword.exe
run=
```

 Note: all files listed on these lines are sep-arated by a single space.

- Check for new drivers for all of your system's components such as video cards, sound cards, mouse driver, etc. Newer drivers are usually faster, smaller and function better than old ones. But be aware that this is not always the case; that's why it's a good idea to keep a copy of old versions in case new ones turn out be duds.

- Load special drivers only when absolutely necessary. For example, most Microsoft-compatible mice work fine with the default Windows mouse driver. If you can use a standard driver, please do.

- Defragment your hard drive. Today, even DOS (version 6.0 and higher) includes a DEFRAG utility that performs this function. There are also numerous third-party defragmentation programs, like Norton's SpeedDisk that can do an even better job. A defragmented hard drive performs faster because all the information for a single file will be stored contiguously, rather than scattered around your drive.

- Keep at least 25M or 10% of your hard drive empty. This leaves ample room for swap files, temporary files, and other work space that programs sometimes need. A full hard drive also runs a bit more slowly than one with open space available. This slowdown occurs because the weight of all that data on the disk slows it down, NOT!—data on a hard drive is just electrons on a magnetic surface. Actually, the speed decreases because of the amount of information that a drive must traverse in order to retrieve a specified file; more data simply means longer average search times. That's why it's a good idea to do some regular housekeeping on your hard disks, and to migrate older, seldom-used files to (well-documented and clearly labeled) tapes or floppies.

- Lower the resolution of your display and use a solid color background, instead of a bitmap for your desktop. While these are subtle (and even boring) changes, they can provide extra boosts of speed to a dragging Windows desktop.

SUMMARY

Optimizing Windows depends primarily on optimizing memory usage, both in the DOS bootup sequence and in your Windows startup. In this chapter, we've covered numerous hints and tips for squeezing the most performance out of your system. But the best—and simplest—summary of everything we've had to say on the subject can be expressed as: "If you don't need it, don't use it!" These are words to live by, especially in the era of RAM cram (trying to shoehorn more drivers, TSRs, etc. into an increasingly crowded conventional memory and UMB address space) and higher memory prices.

Tech Support: They Are There to Help, Right?!

12

In this chapter, we'll discuss how to work with technical support operations to get the answers you want and need. In large part, this consists of knowing in advance what questions to expect, and being prepared to answer them promptly and accurately. Just remember, anything that saves time for the person on the other side of the connection not only saves you time, but can also save you money!

Q1: How do I know that I have a real problem?

Repeatability is the key to a real problem. If you're able to repeat an error, lock-up, reboot, or whatever, then you have a situation that others can reproduce, and hopefully fix on your behalf.

Once you've established that your problem is repeatable, write down the problem and the steps or actions that cause it to occur. Be as specific as possible when stating the problem. Instead of saying, "My CD-ROM doesn't work" say, "When I try to play the CD-ROM based game Flash Traffic, the video segments stutter and have blurs."

The clearer and more precise your problem definition, the easier it will be for your tech support counterparts to find a solution. Likewise, the steps that lead up to your problem should also be specific, for example:

1. I boot computer and start Windows.

2. I insert CD-ROM disc in player.

3. Using the mouse, I click File then Run.

4. I type in box "D:\setup", then press OK with mouse.

5. Welcome screen appears, I click OK to continue.

6. Screen blacks out and system reboots.

This information will be useful to the technical support personnel in replicating the problem, determining its cause, and (hopefully) providing a direct solution or at least, a workaround.

Q2: What should I do before calling tech support?

Before you call tech support, solve your own problem as much as you possibly can. Working through the solutions suggested in this book should cover 95% of the reasons that people call tech support in the first place. Trying to solve your own problem will save you money on long distance charges, and will build your familiarity with your system.

If you've worked through the suggestions in the book, but have found no solutions, you should have developed some definite ideas about where the problem lies, and if it is software- or hardware-related. This information will be very valuable if and when you do make the call to tech support.

Q3: What do I need to know before calling tech support?

There are three things you need to know before calling tech support:

- The Problem—See Q1. A clear and precise explanation of your problem, what steps are required to repeat it, and your ideas about how it may have originated will be the key pieces of information that a good tech support person will request. This information answers the two basic tech support questions: "What happens?" and "When does it occur?"

- Your System—See Chapter 1. You need to know not only the hardware which comprises your system, but also what software is installed, your configuration parameters, and the contents of your startup files for both DOS and Windows. The more information you have about your system that you can explain to the tech support people, the more specific their solutions can be. Therefore, always have your CIF handy when making tech support calls.

- Your Solution—See the rest of this book. One reason you purchased this book was to aid your own troubleshooting efforts, to help prevent unnecessary tech support calls. Most of the information in this book is designed to walk you through solutions to the problems that typically occur when using Multimedia or CD-ROM based software. Before you make any calls to tech support, please take the time to work through the related suggestions listed here. Keep track of what you did and what results from your efforts. If and when you do call tech support, knowing what doesn't work can help you to get to other solutions that may not be listed here, or which are too software or hardware specific for us to mention in any kind of detail (and, we're sorry to say, there are lots of those you'll run into from time to time).

Q4: What do I do as I get ready to call?

Before you ever pick up the phone to dial the hotline number you need to consider a few things, like the following:

- Is this an emergency?

   Calling tech support in an emergency won't often get you a fast solution. Working with support personnel takes time and patience, both of which are usually absent in most emergencies. Unless you can make the time and remain calm, wait until after the emergency's over to call tech support.

- Do you have the time?

   A tech support call can last from 15 minutes to a few hours, with most of this time spent on hold or trapped in a voicemail help database. If you can't afford to stay on the phone until you receive a solution, don't make the call right now. Wait until you'll be ready, able and willing to stay on the phone until you get a solution.

- Are you able to handle the solution?

    If you call tech support for a solution, you need to be prepared to walk through that solution while you're still on the phone. This may mean opening a computer case to move jumpers, flipping through a manual, editing startup files and even repeating the lead-in activities over and over again. Be sure you have a collection of proper tools and the manuals for the system and its software close at hand.

- Will you be distracted?

    Unfortunately, most of your time on the phone will be spent waiting for tech support, not actually talking to someone. But for those few precious moments when you do get to speak with a human, you need to give them your complete and undivided attention (especially since that's what they're giving you). Don't answer other calls, don't talk with people around you, and try not to ask them to hold (even though they may need to place you on hold at times). Also, try to keep your surroundings quiet.

- Are you near the computer?

    Don't ever call tech support if you aren't sitting in front of the computer that's experiencing the problem. Most of the solutions that tech support people suggest require that you follow them step by step, providing feedback and commentary as you perform the suggested tasks. If you're not where the action is, the tech support people can't help very much.

119

- What time zones are you calling?

    Computer product companies are scattered around the globe. Usually the ones you need to call most will be at least 3 times zones away. As you're dialing, realize that you may be calling before they open, during lunch, or after they've closed. It's almost always worth investigating e-mail or faxes as alternatives to the phone!

- Do you have your CIF, a notepad, and a pen handy?

    You will need all the information about your system that is in your CIF. You will need to write down the solutions suggested by the technician. It's also a good idea to document the time and date of the call, and to record the name of the person you speak to; all of this information can come in handy if you ever need to document your efforts to fix the problem (when trying for a refund, or simply when reporting on progress).

- Get a grip!

    You need to understand one important aspect of calling technical support: You won't be talking with the designers or programmers of the software/hardware that's causing your problem. You will be talking with a person, probably from an outside agency, hired to read manuals and search technical databases for possible solutions to your problem. They have no more responsibility for the problems occurring on your system than you have for the War of 1812. Try to make him or her into a partner, not an antagonist!

Q5: When's the best time to call tech support?

The best time to call a tech support line is within the first hour that they start receiving calls. During this hour the staff will typically receive the fewest calls, making it easier for you to get through. Also, the crew will be fresh and easier to work with since they haven't been talking with angry people all day.

The worst times to call tech support are during the last two hours of their workday, or during their lunch breaks. The late part of the day is when most calls come in, forcing hold times way up. Lunch breaks mean fewer support people to answer calls, which also forces hold times to go up. Even during these times you still might get through, but keep a supply of food and water nearby.

Most tech support lines are open from 9 AM to 6 PM in their respective time zones, but very few are open over the weekend. Usually the company will have a recorded message that gives the details for their hours of operation; use this information to plan the right time to call them back. It may mean getting up really early, or staying up really late, but a little planning goes a long way under these circumstances.

Q6: I finally got through to a real person, what should I do?

- Be polite! Tech support staff sit at a computer terminals and answer calls all day long about other people's problems. Usually the people who call are upset, frustrated or even angry. Think about that before you start giving anyone a hard time. You may not be up to laughing with them on the phone, but at least, don't add to their misery by acting like a jerk.

- Speak clearly at a good volume directly into the telephone handset; if you have to use a speakerphone, make sure they can hear you before launching into long-winded explanations (they're a real pain to repeat, as you'll soon learn).

- Answer all questions as directly and specifically as you can. Reference your CIF and your notes as you explain your situation. If you don't know the answer to a question, don't make one up. Tell the person "I don't know;" often, your support technician can walk you through procedures that will give them the answers they need.

- As a solution is being explained, write down the steps required. Add this information to your CIF, in case a similar problem ever recurs.

Q7: What do I do after the call?

If the help you received from a tech support person was thorough, specific and useful, be sure to get their name and extension. Write their employer, and tell them about the good service you received. If you received poor service—which doesn't mean that no solution was found but rather, that the technician was rude, unprofessional or insulting—report that to the company as well.

Q8: What do I do with the solution?

Not every call to a tech support line is like a wish come true. Some problems are stubborn and require extreme measures to repair, overcome, or work around them. Be mentally prepared for any or all of the following tasks, that you may be called on to perform:

- Reconfigure a significant portion of your hardware in order to accommodate an ill-behaved software or hardware product that you just can't live without.

- Retrieve new versions of software or drivers to achieve compatibility and functionality. You will often need access to an on-line service like the Internet or CompuServe, or even the company's BBS system, to get what you need. Sometimes you may even be forced to wait for the vendor to snail mail you the required software, or to be asked to go out to buy something new at your friendly neighborhood computer store.

- Your current system may not support a reasonable solution to your problems. This may force you to try to return the offending product. In many cases, opened software cannot be returned to its place of purchase, so you'll need to mail it back to the manufacturer and wait up to 2 months before receiving a refund check. To do this you'll need a Return Merchandise Authorization (RMA) number, which links your shipment with the company's acceptance of that merchandise and, ultimately, the long-awaited refund. If this procedure is necessary, the support personnel will be able to walk your through their company's regulations regarding returns and refunds.

- Return a defective hardware product: This can often disable your system until a replacement arrives. Even with overnight shipment, this means at least one day of downtime (more, if their shipping department has already closed for the day).

Q9: What if I can't get through to a human?

Many companies are switching to computerized, menu-driven phone help systems to answer more and more of their tech support questions. These systems can be both immediately helpful and downright annoying. The idea of a common solutions database is a good one, but most of the common questions have already been answered here in this book.

Even so, you may still need to peruse these systems for hardware- or software-specific information. We ran across a few companies that didn't make a full time technician available by phone, where the only way to get answers was through the computer menu system or by leaving a voice mail message.

The single most beneficial aspect of a computer phone menu system is that it's available 24 hours a day. It may be worth a few minutes to search the database for an answer before getting into the ever-popular queue to wait for a human technician. Remember, 99.99% of the tech problems you encounter have already been experienced by someone else. If they called tech support, it's probably listed in the computer database. All you have to save (and lose) is your own sweet time!

Q10: I don't want to get stuck in "hold hell" waiting for a technician on the phone. Are there other ways to get technical support without waiting forever?

Yes. You can try locating the software or hardware manufacturer on one of the popular on-line services (e.g., CompuServe, the Internet, etc.). Often, you'll be able to access e-mail support, review on-line documentation, or even examine the list of current patches, drivers, fixes and upgrades that are available. Best of all, you can download whatever you think you might need right away, at minimal expense with very little waiting (unless the files are truly huge; be warned, this does occasionally happen!)

On the Internet, you'll need to run a search using one of the following Web sites:

```
Yahoo -
http://www.yahoo.com/
```

or

```
WebCrawler -
http://webcrawler.cs.washington.edu/WebCrawler/
```

You might need to root around a bit to locate what you want, but these two sites are by far the most helpful in locating resources. Try to use the company's name, its acronym, or even the software or hardware product's name for searching.

On CompuServe you can use WinCIM's Find feature to look for companies or products. You can also write for help in one of the forums. There are numerous file locator programs available as well; for the PC the best one is the PC File Finder (GO PCFF) which you can search by file type, file name, category, or keywords. This can turn up necessary items quickly and easily.

Some companies also offer BBS systems that can supply technical information; often these numbers are listed in their product documentation. If you aren't familiar with BBS systems or modem communications, you'll need to call a human answering tech support line instead. You might want to consider investing the effort necessary to master these tools, however, because they can provide invaluable sources of inspiration and information in your quest for technical help.

SUMMARY

Technical support is another tool that you need to learn how to use; approached properly, technical support operations can make the difference between success and failure, or between slow, inefficient operations and finely-tuned, high-performance computing. Here, as elsewhere in life, be sure to get the right tools for the job. If you use your technical support tools properly and take good care of them (especially your CIF), they will make your life easier, happier, and more productive. What more could you want?

RDA— Recommended minimum configurAtion

13

In this chapter, we'll present our opinions on the minimum requirements for a workable multimedia CD-ROM system. You'll find that we differ somewhat from the recommendations that you'll hear from vendors (especially from the Multimedia PC vendors association, also known as MPC or MPC2); don't worry, we'll try to explain why we differ, or at least what our recommendations will buy you.

> **Q1: What's a good PC system configuration for running multimedia and CD-ROM based software?**

Based on our experience and testing work with over 150 multimedia and CD-ROM software packages, we have found the following configuration to be an acceptable configuration for a multimedia system. This is our version of a working model, not the ultimate "dream machine."

- CPU: 486DX33: Provides adequate process speed and gives the added benefits of a built in math co-processor. The faster your chip, the better your system's performance will be. Stay with clock speed multiples of 33; avoid those of 25. Also, avoid true 50 MHz chips if at all possible; they aren't compatible with the VESA Standards used in VLB BIOS cards (we found this out the hard way.)

- 8M RAM 70ns: This supplies enough room for most software, at a speed that should not limit the CPU. If you have the bucks, get 16M at 60ns; then, you will be able to really blaze along. No matter what, do not settle for 4M. See Chapter 4 for more details.

- A VLB motherboard: A VLB MB can communicate at 33 MHz, or at a speed that's compatible with the recommended CPUs. It also offers an excellent choice of high-speed peripheral cards (video, disk controller, etc.) with a good price/performance tradeoff. Otherwise, consider a PCI motherboard; they're a bit more expensive, but faster, and will support more high-speed peripheral devices than VLB (5 vs. 2).

- VLB 2M VRAM Video Card with 16.7 million colors: This is a must for multimedia, and will provide all the speed, clarity and crispness you might want. As a higher-cost alternative, consider an equivalent PCI video card; see Chapter 5 for more details.

- 15" Monitor, SVGA 1024x768, Non-Interlaced: This kind of monitor will adequately meet most needs, but if you can afford the additional costs, go for the gusto, and get a 17" monitor (or larger). More real estate on your screen means more productivity (and more fun playing games).

- 16 bit sound card with MIDI and wavetable synthesis: You'll also need speakers with built-in amplifiers, or a hook-up to your stereo system. Without sound, multimedia is as dull as a popup book with all the pop-ups missing. Without meaning to endorse a single company, the Sound Blaster remains the most reliable and compatible sound card on the market. See Chapter 3 for more information.

- VLB IO card: This must include at least one 16550 UART chip and be able to control 2 IDE hard drives, 2 floppies, 2 serial ports, 1 parallel port and a game port (if your sound card does not have one). Since this is the control center for all data that enters or leaves your system, it's not a bad place to invest a few extra bucks, either.

- 420M IDE hard drive: This should be enough room for a few good software packages, as long as you keep things orderly and remove stuff you no longer use. Remember that you can always add another IDE, swap out a smaller drive for a larger one, or add SCSI hard drives out the wazoo. Disk space is like money: You can never have too much!!

- 3X Spin CD-ROM drive: Internal, without a caddy (unless you want to tip him). A triple spin will keep you ahead of MPC level 2 specifications. We lean toward the NEC line, but Sony and TEAC have great models as well. See Chapter 2 for more CD-ROM recommendations.

- Adaptec 1542 SCSI card: Only if the CD-ROM is not a proprietary IDE or a SB interface. Adaptec controllers, in our opinion, always seem to perform better than average, and are compatible with most brands of CD-ROM hardware, disk drives, scanners, or other SCSI devices.

- 28,800 BPS V.34 External modem: You'll only need a modem for on-line communications or for playing head to head on-line games. Without a modem, you won't get plugged into the emerging Information Superhighway very easily. In this arena, US Robotics and Practical Peripherals are neck and neck, but far outpace most other options. See Chapter 7 for more modem insights and information.

- And the rest: a 3.5" Floppy drive, a Microsoft-compatible mouse, a 101-key keyboard, and a mid-range joystick. See Chapter 6 for explanations and more details.

Q2: What is a good software base upon which to configure a multimedia environment?

- MS DOS 6.22: This version has proven itself to be the latest and greatest edition of the original PC Disk Operating System. With its many upgrades and enhancements, its utilities are both powerful and useful.
- Microsoft Windows 3.11: Still not perfect, but without a doubt the best interface and environment for the PC going. The Windows for Workgroups version is a little buggy for non-networked users, but the 3.11 version takes its most useful features and adds them to the 3.1 edition, creating an improved 3.11.

   Although we've heard good reports about Windows 95, and have experienced mixed results in our testing and experimentation, we haven't had the luxury of testing the final commercial release. Based on what we've seen so far, we're still a little nervous about switching our production machines over to its first release. With a bug-fix upgrade in the offing for the year's (1995's) end, we'll probably wait and switch later!

- QuarterDeck's QEMM: One of the best memory manager tools on the market. QEMM has the amazing ability to use extended memory to load many drivers; on most of our systems it has opened up 634K of conventional memory for application use (618K for DOS sessions under Windows). See Chapters 4 and 10 for more information about memory management and its positive potential side effects.

- Helix Software's Multimedia Cloaking: A great companion to most memory managers, this software is especially useful for multimedia systems. On several of our systems, it lets us load a memory cache, a mouse driver, and a special version of the Microsoft CD-ROM extensions (MSCDEX.EXE) above the 1 MB high-water mark!

These four software packages, properly installed, use their own built in optimization utilities. They can prepare your system for outstanding multimedia performance.

SUMMARY

Our recommended system should be able to provide its owner with limitless possibilities for multimedia interaction. But these are only our suggested minimums, and as stated elsewhere in the book numerous times, if you manage to do better than the minimum, you should always be pleased with the results.

Drop the Dead Donkey!

14

In this chapter, we'll discuss the assumptions we've made about you, the readers of this book. Hopefully, if you know what we've assumed, this will aid you in getting the most out of our answers to your questions. It should also prevent us from making donkeys of ourselves, so to speak (ASSUME = ASS + U + ME).

Q1: What were the authors' basic assumptions?

Here they are. Throughout this book, right or wrong, we've assumed the following about our readers:

- That our readers are human (what else would you be?)

- That our readers can read English (are you following us?)

- That our readers can follow directions (touch your right index finger to the tip of your nose).

- That our readers can consult their manuals for installation instructions (you have kept them all, haven't you?)

- That our readers use and/or own a computer, and are basically familiar with its use (why else would you care about making a CD-ROM work?).

- That our readers are familiar with standard computer terminology (like DOS, CD-ROM, and VGA, etc.).

- That our readers are smart enough to know when they don't know something. (This is our biggest assumption).

Q2: What software version assumptions did we make?

- That you're using DOS 5.0 or later
- That you're using Windows 3.1 or later

If the suggestions we offer don't produce the desired results, you might want to verify that you're working in an environment that matches these assumptions. If not, that could very well explain any discrepancies.

Q3: Did you assume we could edit a file?

Yes, we assume that you know how to use EDIT from the DOS prompt, or Notepad within Windows. Both of these programs are basic text editors, and you should become familiar with them if you aren't already. You can obtain information about their use from your own computer, as follows:

- EDIT: from a DOS prompt, HELP EDIT<ENTER>

- Notepad: from Windows, Select File Run then type NOTEPAD<ENTER>. Then select Help Contents.

While neither program's online help is a marvel of modern communications, each is adequate to instruct you about its program's basic operations. Try them, and see!

> **Q4: Did you assume we knew how to make a backup, and restore data from backups?**

Emphatically, YES! If you have a specialty tape or drive system with backup software, you'll need to spend time learning how to use it. Be sure you know if it runs from both DOS and Windows. If your backup works only in Windows, what will you do when Windows breaks? (Hint: get one that works in both environments; it'll make recovery from a catastrophe that much easier).

If you don't have a third-party backup system, you can still make reliable backups with the DOS MSBACKUP.EXE program. MSBACKUP is a small but effective program that will back up and restore one file or an entire hard drive. MSBACKUP can operate from the DOS prompt or from an enhanced version in Windows.

Take the time necessary to familiarize yourself with your backup program of choice, and its use. Make a few test backups and restorations to be sure you can rely on this system should you ever find yourself in dire straits.

For the built-in DOS backup program, you can run it from DOS by typing: MSBACKUP<ENTER>. After it scans your hard drive, you'll be presented with an options screen. You can get help by pressing ALT-H, or using the mouse and clicking on HELP. If you're using a third-party backup package, read the fabulous manual (RTFM) that came with the product, and familiarize yourself with it, instead.

Before you make a backup of your 500m hard drive to 500 or so floppies, you should consider the options for making a system backup.

- You can either back up each and every file on your drive(s), or you can select only those files that contain configuration information, or data which isn't present on the installation disks, and therefore needs to be saved.

- You can make a full backup onto floppies and find a warehouse to store the hundreds of diskettes it can take, or you can use a small box of disks when you only back up data and configuration files.

- If you want a one step return to normalcy, then a full backup is the key; but if you don't mind re-installing all your software, and then restoring your backed-up data and configuration files, a selective backup is in order.

- You can back up to the same or a different hard drive, to floppy disks, or even to a tape drive.

Whichever way you choose to make backups, always write down what you did, when you did it and how to restore the system. It may seem obvious now, but will it be as transparent at 3 AM the night before your project is due? Remember, the job you save may be your own!

Q5: Did you assume we would read the glossary?

Yes. We wrote the glossary in a special format to make it interesting, and to provide you with as much useful information as possible. The more you know about your computer, the more productive and useful it will become. Therefore, the more you know about computer jargon—which is what the glossary is intended to explore and explain—the better you'll be able to understand what your computer is doing (or not doing) at any given moment.

Q6: Did you assume we would read Chapter 1?

Yes, Chapter 1 is the most important chapter in this book. Most of your problems can be solved or removed if you'll follow and employ the information contained in that chapter. Take the time to read it, even if it's for the second time. You might also notice the repeated use of our favorite word, BACKUP. You might even decide to follow our advice, and perform regular backups of your very own!

SUMMARY

In this chapter, we've tried to tell you what we think you know and don't know, and what aspects of the computer universe you may have visited before, however briefly. Knowing that making assumptions is always fraught with peril, we've shared these assumptions with you so that you'll understand what kind of deck we're dealing this information from (hey, where's that Queen of Spades?)

The Windows 95 Experience

15

In this chapter, we'll discuss the new version of Microsoft's "Integrated Operating System"—Windows 95 and how it handles multimedia. Our first impression can be summed up in one word: WOW!

 Note: *Our research is a compilation of materials gathered from:*

1. *previews of the Win 95 August 24th release*
2. *notes and messages on-line*
3. *our own hands-on experience with Beta build 480.*

Therefore, some specifics listed below may be altered or changed in the final release of Win 95.

> **Q1: What can I do to optimize the use of my CD-ROM in Win 95?**

Most of the controls for your CD-ROM can be adjusted in the File System Properties folder. Getting there is a little tricky but here goes:

- Start Button - Settings - Control Panel

- select System; select the Performance tab, then the File System... button

- finally the CD-ROM tab of the File System Properties window. In this window, you can adjust the size of the cache used for the CD-ROM.

Also, there are five preset read patterns, use each to determine which works best for your system. Don't be afraid to use the Quad Speed setting if your CD-ROM player is only a Double Speed machine. This has been known to be the optimal setting for some systems, despite the apparent discrepancy.

Q2: I have an IDE CD-ROM drive or another non-standard interface CD-ROM drive which does not seem to work with Win 95. What can I do?

Windows 95 is a new standard for device drivers, as Windows 3.1 once was. Most manufacturers are rushing to adapt their drivers to make them Win 95 compliant. If your CD-ROM—or any other hardware device for that matter—isn't automatically configured when you install Win 95, don't fret; all you need is an updated driver. You can run down Win 95 drivers for your hardware devices in any of several possible ways:

- Contact Microsoft by means of the World Wide Web (http://www.microsoft.com) and search their software library for driver updates.

- Contact the product's manufacturer. If they don't have a Win 95 driver patch yet, they should be able to tell you when it will be available. Be sure to get specific information about where to find the file, and how to retrieve it when it is released.

- Search CompuServe or the Internet for drivers. Look in software archives, the company's Web pages or forums, and in special Win 95 focus areas. (Note: there should be plenty of the latter around by the time you read this.)

Q3: I retrieved a new driver to allow my old hardware to work under Win 95. How can I install this driver?

Win 95 is very close to true Plug-n-Play technology. Microsoft has included a hardware installation wizard that walks you through the driver/software installation process. It works something like this:

- Use Start to get to Control Panel; notice the folders that show up.

- Select the Add New Hardware folder (looks like an icon).

- Since you're going to add New Hardware, you'll see a single Click Next> button (it's the first page of the installation wizard you're using).

- The second page will feature a radio button to search your systems for new hardware. Because you already know that this hardware is not defined, select the NO radio button.

- Then click the Next> button; this flips you to the

next page, where you'll be able to enter information about your new hardware.

- From here you will be able to select the type of hardware that you want to add a driver for. (Note: you may be able to skip this step if you already have the drivers you need, and don't have to retrieve them from the Win 95 CD.)

- Finally, you can load the new driver using the Have Disk... button.

If you have difficulty installing a new driver, you'll need to contact the manufacturer and make sure that you've obtained the correct version of the driver. Otherwise, you may have to go online or obtain a copy right from the manufacturer to proceed to install the latest and greatest version.

Q4: How can I install a new software package on Windows 95?

You can install most DOS or Windows software packages on Windows 95 by using their prepackaged installation utilities. Here's how:

- Place the installation disk in the appropriate drive

- Use the Start button; and click Run...

- Locate the drive and select the appropriate installation program.

- Run the installation program, and follow its instructions faithfully!

After you've finished the installation, you have many options for executing your newly installed software. Here are just a few:

- Use Start, click Run... then type the file's full path or look for it with the Browse... button.

- Use Start, click Find...; Files or Folders...; use the Name and Location tab to search for the file using the file name. Double click on the right one to execute it.

- Use Windows Explorer or My Computer to locate the file and double click or use File Open to execute it.

- Create a desktop shortcut. Right click on the open desktop, select New then Shortcut. Use the Browse... button to search for the start file. This wizard will help you create a new icon on the desktop which you can double click to run your software.

- Add the new software to the Start menu. Right click on an empty area of the Taskbar, select Properties, select the tab labeled Start Menu Programs, then the Add... button. Follow the instructions given to add the program, a name, an icon and designate it's location in the hierarchy.

If you don't want to run the program using one of these methods, figure out your own method. From what we've seen of Windows 95, there's definitely more than one way to skin this particular cat!

Q5: What is the best place to get help or other information about Windows 95?

The best place to get information about Win 95 is directly from Microsoft. In fact, the company has a World Wide Web site dedicated to Windows 95. It's located at http://www.microsoft.com. Microsoft also has a forum on CompuServe where you can find Win 95 information, using WinCIM: GO MICROSOFT. Or, you can try the FIND command, and supply "Windows 95" as the argument (by the time you read this, these keywords should produce a multitude of hopefully helpful forms and resources with information about Windows 95).

There is a plethora of Internet sites popping up that are focused on Win 95. Most of these are run by end-users, programmers or even a few hackers, who are looking to get all they can out of Win 95. To get started in your quest for these non-Microsoft sites, use the Web search engines like Yahoo or WebCrawler to search for "Windows 95".

You'll find add-ons, work-arounds, short-cuts, hints and tips, and even 32-bit betas of many programs. Take the time to explore and experiment, but remember to make backups of your old configuration before you wreak too much havoc on your system. It pays to be able to get back to where you started, especially when the "new and improved" tends towards the "bizarre and flaky."

Q6: Will my DOS and Windows 3.1 software work under Windows 95?

Quite amazingly, the answer to this question is "Yes."Most PC software functions under Windows 95, although a little tweaking of a startup or a .PIF file may be required to get things working smoothly. If you have difficulty running a software package under Windows 95, try any or all of the following tips:

- For a DOS program, use My Computer to locate the start file for the software,
  - Select File Properties.
  - Select the Program tab then the Advanced... button. Here you can select MS-DOS mode and configure a specific DOS environment for the software.

 Note: *when you try to run software in MS-DOS mode, you will have to close all other programs currently open. Win 95 will reboot your machine using the new start-up parameters you designed, then auto-matically load the program. After you have finished using the program, your system will re-boot again back to Win 95. Be careful to include everything you will need in the startup files, especially SCSI, sound, video and memory drivers.*

- Try to re-install the software, especially if you did not use Win 95 to install it in the first place.

- Try to use a DOS installation utility instead of the Windows utility, if A DOS installation utility is available.

- Contact the manufacturer for the steps required to make the software function under Win 95. This may include .PIF editing, changing .INI files, retrieving patches or fixes, or even purchasing an upgrade.

- Search the Internet or CompuServe for informa-tion about the software in question and its relationship to Windows 95. You may be surprised by what you learn! You may also benefit from the experience of other people who have been where you're trying to go.

Q7: What other multimedia controls does Win 95 have?

Win 95 includes numerous built-in multimedia controls. One way to access these controls is to use the media player. Do this by using Start; Programs; Accessories; Multimedia; Media Player. In media player, select the Device type, then Device Properties. Depending on which media type you select, you can adjust the system to your liking. There is also a multi-channel volume mixer available; you can get to it through Device; Volume Control.

More controls are available through the Control Panel. You can get there by using Start; Settings; Control Panel. Look in the Multimedia and the System folders for multimedia controls that you can adjust.

SUMMARY

In this chapter, we took a brief look at the wonderful new version of Windows, Windows 95. At first blush, it seems easier to configure and manipulate its environment to suit your needs, particularly for multimedia, when compared to earlier Windows implementations.

But, as with any new operating environment, you should test everything more than once, following different orders each time you test. You need to become thoroughly familiar with a new system before you can start relying on it for production work. In addition to its considerable capabilities and improvements, we also feel that there's a steep learning curve for Windows 95, both for amateur as well as professional computer users.

Part II

The Macintosh Multimedia Experience

Macintosh Multimedia Madness: In the Beginning

16

We'd like to begin by congratulating you on your choice of multimedia computers. Macs are generally better multimedia computers than PCs. More importantly, Mac CD-ROM titles are much more likely to work the first time you try them. PC CD-ROMs have many more things that can go wrong (as you can see by the relative number of pages devoted to each platform in this book).

While Macs are easier, they're not perfect. There are still things that can and do go wrong. Most are easy to fix. So sit back, relax, and we'll cover them all in a few blessedly brief chapters.

In this first chapter we'll look at some issues that should be dealt with before you even stick in a CD-ROM disc.

> **Q1: The CD-ROMs outer box lists all these Minimum Hardware Requirements: 68020 or higher, 256 colors, System 7, 8 megs of RAM, 10Mb hard disk space available. How do I find out what MY Mac has?**

You probably know what processor is inside your Mac, a 68020, 68030, 68040, PowerPC 601, etc. If you don't, check the Technical Information booklet that came with your system. (Worst case: call your dealer or Apple.)

You probably know whether you have a color monitor or not (if you have a color monitor, you probably have at least 256 colors). If you aren't sure, open the Monitors control panel. (Choose Control Panels from the Apple menu, then open the Monitors icon.) You will see a list of colors: Black & White, 4, 16, 256, Thousands, Millions, etc. The highest one you see in the list is the highest number your Mac supports.

To learn which version of the System software you're running, as well as how much RAM (Random Access Memory) your Mac has, open About This Macintosh (see Figure 16.1). You'll find it under the Finders Apple menu. The Finder is where your hard disk and CD-ROM icons live. If you're in the Finder, you should see your hard disk icon, the Trash can, etc. If you're not in the Finder (i.e. you're using another program), choose Finder from the application menu in the upper right-hand corner of your screen. Then choose About This Macintosh from the Apple menu in the upper left corner. The About This Macintosh window appears:

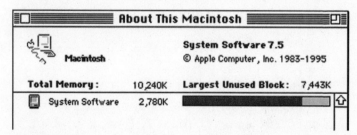

Figure 16.1 About This Macintosh tells you a lot about your Mac.

18 items	884 MB in disk	112.7 MB available
Name		Size Kind

Figure 16.2 Now you know how much room is left on your hard disk (112.7 megabytes).

The About This Macintosh window tells you what version of the System Software you're running (System Software 7.5), how much RAM your Mac has (10,240, more commonly called 10 megs or 10 megabytes), and how much RAM is available for programs (also known as the Largest Unused Block, 7,443K in Figure 16.1).

To find out how much hard disk space you have left, open the Views control panel and click the Show Disk Info in Header checkbox. An X should appear in the box if it didn't, click the box again. Close the Views control panel. Now open any window in the Finder, your hard disk, a folder, a CD, whatever.

Now all of your windows display available disk space (112.7 megs), the number of items currently displayed in that window (18 in Figure 16.2), and how much stuff is already on that disk (a whopping 884 MB).

Q2: What is the difference between System 6 and System 7? Can I still run multimedia titles if my Mac has System 6 on it?

You may be able to, but many of the best titles require the newer (and, in our opinion, better) System 7.X (System 7, System 7.0.1, System 7.1, System 7.5, are collectively referred to as System 7.X.) In fact, the rest of this book assumes you're running some variant of System 7.

If your System Software version number doesn't have a 7 in it, and you're serious about multimedia, you ought to move up to System 7.5, which is much more multimedia friendly than any previous version. Call your Apple dealer, or MacConnection or Mac-Warehouse for an upgrade.

Here's one more gotcha: Though most boxes don't mention it, many games won't play on a 12 monitor! If you have a 12 monitor, our advice is never to buy a CD-ROM from anyplace that won't take it back if it doesn't work.

Extension & Control Panel Management: You Turn Me On (and Off)

Extensions and Control Panels are special Mac- intosh files that load themselves when your Mac starts up. Mostly extensions and control panels are helpful. But sometimes one or more of them interferes with your CD-ROM enjoyment. And, since many of them use up precious RAM when they load, it's good to know how to manage them.

> **Q3: The Minimum System Requirements for the game are at least 4 Mb of RAM. About This Macintosh says I have more than 4 Mb of RAM available. I get a Not Enough Memory error when I try to play. Why?**

Chances are you've got a bunch of extensions and control panels loading at startup, hogging up your RAM. Our calls to various tech support hot-lines revealed that this is the most common cause of problems!

Here's the cure: Disable all extensions and control panels except those needed to use a CD-ROM.

If you're using System 7.5.X: It's easy to disable unneeded extensions and control panels using System 7.5's Extensions Manager control panel. (This is yet another great reason to upgrade to System 7.5.) Open the Extensions Manager control panel now (see Figure 16.3). Click the pop-up Sets menu and select Save Set. Name it My Regular Set. That will let you put things back the way they were when you're done running your CD-ROM title.

Next, turn off (click its name until no checkmark appears to the left of it; see Figure 16.3) everything except:

Apple CD-ROM

Foreign File Access

QuickTime

QuickTime PowerPlug (if you're on a Power Mac)

Sound Manager

Click the pop-up Sets menu again and save this set as CD-ROM Only Set. These are the only extensions that need to load in order for your CD-ROM drive to work properly. All others are extraneous. Close the Extensions Manager control panel and restart your Mac so the changes take effect.

This configuration leaves the most possible memory for your CD-ROM title. To restore things to the

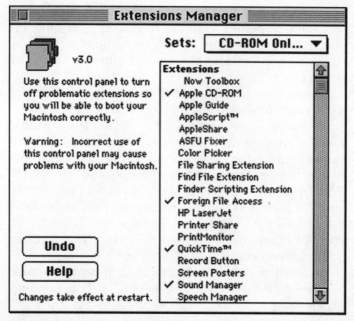

Figure 16.3 This CD-ROM Only set insures your Mac is optimized for playing CD-ROM titles.

way they were, choose the My Regular Set set in the Extensions Manager control panel, close Extensions Manager, then restart.

If you have an earlier version of System 7: It's much more of a hassle, but once you've done it a few times, it'll come naturally. Here's what to do to disable unneeded extensions and control panels manually:

Create a New Folder on your desktop and call it disabled stuff. Open the Control Panels folder (in your System Folder) and drag everything in it except the Sound control panel into the disabled stuff folder. Now open the Extensions folder and drag everything in it except:

Apple CD-ROM

Apple Photo Access (if you plan to use PhotoCDs)

Foreign File Access

High Sierra File Access

ISO 9660 File Access

QuickTime

QuickTime PowerPlug (if you're on a Power Mac)

Now restart your Mac. This lean, mean configuration leaves the most possible memory available for your CD-ROM title.

To set things back the way they were, open the disabled stuff folder and select everything in it (use the keyboard shortcut Command-A). Drag all these icons onto the System Folder icon and release the mouse button. A dialog box will ask you if it's OK to put them in their proper places. It is. Things are now back the way they were.

If you bought your CD-ROM drive separately from your Mac, there's a good chance your CD-ROM drive uses software other than the Apple CD-ROM extension. If you have a third-party CD-ROM drive, check your documentation and substitute the name of the CD-ROM extension supplied with your drive for Apple CD-ROM in the above paragraphs. Also, if you have a third-party drive and it came with its own extension, make sure you're not also loading the Apple CD-ROM extension. It's one or the other, but never load both.

If this doesn't free up enough memory to allow you to successfully run the CD-ROM title, you may need to lower your Disk Cache setting as well (see the tip in Chapter 20).

Backing Up is Hard To Do
(Do It Anyway)

OK. So now you know everything you could possibly want to know about your Mac. You're ready to sally forth and plop in a disc. Not so fast, bucko! You're about to INSTALL SOFTWARE. And many CD-ROM titles today install stuff in your all-important SYSTEM FOLDER. If something should go wrong after installing this new software, can you put your System Folder back just like it was?

The answer is, not if you don't have a backup. If you make a backup before installing anything new, you can restore those files if they're overwritten or damaged during the upgrade process (or if you decide you like the old version better).

 Warning: If you fail to back up before installing any new software, you run the risk of losing important files. If you lose data files, they'll stay lost. Never, never, never keep the only copy of a data file on your hard drive. Don't even keep the backup on the same hard drive. Whenever possible make a floppy or tape backup of your data files. The only way to restore data correctly is to restore it from a backup.

If you don't have backup software already, get some. We can't stress this strongly enough. If you don't have a complete backup of your System Folder and important documents, you're an accident waiting to happen. You will eventually lose data and probably pay someone a lot of money to try, perhaps unsuccessfully, to get it back for you.

This book isn't the place for a tutorial on good

backup habits, but, as always, we recommend strongly that you backup important files often.

What Installers Do

Q4: Most games have an Installer. What exactly is it doing?

Most games these days have an Installer program. At the very least, it will install a folder and/or one or more files on your hard disk. Some Installers are smart and install QuickTime or the Sound control panel if they don't find them in your extensions (QuickTime) or control panels (Sound) folder at the time of installation.

Many Installers offer two or more installation options based on how much hard disk space you can spare for the game—small, medium, or large installs. The larger installs always perform better; we recommend them if you have the hard disk space available.

Before running the Installer on a new disc, we strongly recommend you read the manual and any Read Me files you find on the disk itself.

Q5: What if I don't have enough space on my hard disk for even the smallest install?

CD-ROM titles eventually take a toll on your hard disk space. Each one wants to install 4, 5, 10, or even 30 megabytes of files! You could always buy a bigger hard disk, but here's a better idea.

When you find yourself running out of space on your hard disk, delete all the old, rarely-played CD-ROM titles from your hard disk. If you haven't played it in the past two weeks, chuck it. You can always reinstall it another time.

To find out how much space you'll regain when you delete a file or folder, click once on its icon to select it, then choose Get Info from the File menu (or use its keyboard shortcut Command-I).

To delete a file or folder, drag it to the Trash, then choose Empty Trash from the Special menu.

CDs and CD-ROM Drives— How to Become a Spin Doctor

17

In this chapter, we'll discuss problems and difficulties that you might encounter with your CD-ROM drive itself, or problems that appear to be stemming from the drive.

> **Q1: I don't see the CD-ROM's icon on the desktop when I insert it.**

A few quick thoughts:

The CD in your drive is upside down (i.e. the label is facing down).

Your external drive doesn't have power or isn't turned on.

The disc caddy is seated or inserted incorrectly.

The disc tray is mis-aligned or not in all the way.

The CD is for a different computer type (e.g., you're trying to read a PC disc).

Try another CD—you may have a badly-produced or defective disc.

If it's none of the above, it could be your CD-ROM driver software. Your CD-ROM drive requires certain extensions to load at startup. More specifically, the Apple CD-ROM, Apple Photo Access, Foreign File Access, High Sierra File Access, and ISO 9660 File Access extensions must be in your Extensions folder or your Mac won't be able to read CD-ROM discs. (If you're trying to listen to an Audio CD, you'll also need the AppleCD Audio Player desk accessory, which should appear under your Apple menu.)

If you don't see them in your Extensions folder or Apple menu, reinstall the System software from your master System Software disks, then restart your Mac to activate them.

If you purchased your CD-ROM drive from someone other than Apple, you should have received software for it on a floppy disk. You should install that instead of the Apple software.

If it's not software, the first thing to try, (which is a good idea each and every single time you encounter any problem whatsoever on your Mac, by the way), is to restart your Mac. Quit all programs, choose Shut Down from the Finder's Special menu, wait for a few minutes, then power your Mac back up. If your CD-ROM drive is external (in its own box, not built into your Mac), be sure to turn its power off for a few seconds, too. Now try again.

If that doesn't work, Shut Down again, turn off your CD-ROM drive (if it's external), and disconnect and reconnect all the cable and power connections. Try again.

Don't forget to try at least one disc other than the one that's giving you problems; if that disc is defective, it can make your CD-ROM appear inoperative when it's working fine (but the disc isn't).

If you're still stuck, the next question to ask is: Have you installed any new hardware lately? If you've recently added a device to your SCSI chain (that's anything in the daisy-chain of devices connected to the SCSI port on your Mac), try disconnecting everything but the CD-ROM drive from the chain. Now retest the CD-ROM.

If you have the same problem even when the CD-ROM drive is the only external device connected, you may have a bad cable. Try another cable. Or a termination problem (see next question).

If it works, but only when it's the only device in the SCSI chain, read on!

Q2: The CD-ROM works if it's the only device in the chain, but not if I connect another drive.

If the CD-ROM drive works when it's the only device connected but not when other devices are in the chain, it could one of several things: a SCSI ID conflict, a bad cable, or a termination issue.

External SCSI devices each take an ID number from 1-6 (there should be a little dial, or button on the back of your external hard disk or CD-ROM drive that displays the SCSI ID number). No two devices can have the same number. IF YOU GIVE TWO EXTERNAL SCSI DEVICES THE SAME NUMBER, VERY, VERY BAD THINGS CAN HAPPEN! That's called a SCSI ID conflict. If two of your devices have the same number, change one of them by clicking the button or turning the wheel, but don't restart your Mac until every device has a unique SCSI ID number.

Or, it could be the cable. Try another cable (note

that this isn't the same cable as before—the first cable was a 25 to 50 pin cable, with one small connector that goes into your Mac and one large connector that goes into your CD-ROM drive; this one has two large 50 to 50 pin connectors, for connecting your CD-ROM drive to another device in the chain).

The last thing it could be, if it wasn't either of the first two, is a matter of SCSI termination. The last device in your SCSI chain must be terminated. What does that mean? It's not important. The only part you need to know is that if the last device in the SCSI chain isn't terminated, your CD-ROM drive (or other SCSI devices) may not work properly.

Many CD-ROM drives (and other external SCSI devices) include internal termination. Consult your documentation and place the terminated device last in your SCSI chain. If none of your devices has termination, you'll have to purchase an external terminator. Call your hard disk or CD-ROM manufacturer, or a mail-order house, and ask for a 50-pin external SCSI terminator.

> **Q3: I just changed discs, why do I still see the grayed-out icon for the previous disc?**

You used the Eject Disk (Command-E) command. It ejects the disk but doesn't dismount it. This is handy when you're copying from one floppy to another or installing from multiple floppy disks, but a bummer for CD-ROMs.

For now, drag the grayed-out icon into the Trash. To avoid this dilemma in the future, eject CD-ROM disks by either dragging their disc icons to the Trash, or selecting the CD-ROMs icon then choosing Put Away (Command-Y) in the File menu.

Hot tip: *If your Mac keeps asking for a disk or disks, try pressing Command-. (that's Command-period) a few times.*

Q4: My CD has dirt, finger prints or dust on the data surface. How should I clean it?

First, let's discuss how to prevent this from happening again:

- Always store CDs in jewel boxes or non-scratch CD sleeves. **Never, never, never** lay a CD down unless it's inside a jewel box, sleeve or caddy.

- Always hold a CD by its edges. You can even put a finger in the center hole if you have small hands.

- Keep your computer area clean and free of food and drink.

- Keep monkeys and farm animals under close supervision when using your computer.

To clean a disc:

- Use only a soft, lint-free cloth. Never use a towel, paper cloth or even your shirt because these materials are abrasive and can scratch the disc. Use a record-cleaning, CD-cleaning, or gold polishing cloth.

- When cleaning, use radial strokes from the center to the outside edge. Never use circular motions; if you do scratch the disc while cleaning, radial scratches can often be corrected by the CD-ROM reader (see Question 5).

- Only use a CD-approved solvent or cleanser. Spray a disc and let it sit for a few minutes, but NEVER RUB OR SCRUB!!! Using radial strokes, wipe off the cleanser. Repeat this until the disc is clean.

- Dust can be removed easily with a can of compressed air. Be sure to get a dust removal can, and not the freeze spray for gum removal. Use short bursts aimed from the center to the edge.

- There are little machines designed to clean CD-ROMs; most of these are designed to provide the radial cleaning action and include a cleansing fluid. Use them with care and caution.

Q5: AARRGGHH! My disc has scratches, is there any hope?

Scratches can make a disc useless. However, a few scratches don't automatically make it unreadable. Most discs are designed with an ECC (Error Correction Code). ECC is a method of recording the data redundantly on the CD; this allows a CD-ROM drive to reconstruct the data which is unreadable under a scratch, from the surrounding data. ECC can overcome some surface flaws, but preventative care is always preferable.

There are a few options to repair scratches, but these should be employed cautiously, and they are listed in the order of the level of damage they can repair, or the damage they can cause if mis-used.

Only try this stuff if the CD-ROM is hosed anyway and there's no other choice.

- CD Polish can remove small scratches. This product is available at most audio CD stores or through music magazines.

- Liquid metal polishes, like Brasso, can fill in small scratches. Use these sparingly!

- Toothpaste, yes toothpaste, a brand made for polishing teeth. Using your finger and a small amount of toothpaste, gently polish away the scratch using radial reciprocating strokes. Use warm water to rinse the CD. Use CD Polish to smooth the scratches the toothpaste caused. Be sure that you understand you will be making scratches to fix a scratch.

- Commercial/Professional Plastic Polishing techniques. This is the method of using fine abrasive paper and liquid polish. Most plastic supply companies have these materials and can give you detailed instructions. Use this only as a last resort.

Q6: My CD-ROM seems to read discs poorly. Can I fix this?

Yes, this is often caused by a dirty lens. First try using compressed air to dust the lens. Then try using a soft Q-tip and rubbing alcohol to gently shine the lens. Some audio CD stores sell lens-cleaning systems, these may also be employed on your Mac's CD-ROM player.

Try other CDs in the drive. If you still experience poor disc reads, call the CD-ROM manufacturer or return the product to its place of purchase; you may have a damaged drive. If it's still under warranty, you may be able to obtain a replacement at low or no cost.

Q7: I bought a new Quad or Hex spin CD-ROM drive, but my programs don't seem to run any faster. Why?

The increased speed of the new higher-spin drives has yet to be exploited by CD-ROM disc publishers. Most software packages are designed to run on double-speed drives; therefore, they only require a 300KB per second transfer rate. On a triple spin device, video and audio quality is often increased, but rarely will the software take full advantage of the 450Kbps transfer rate. Generally, most software on the shelves today won't run any faster on a Hex spin than on a triple or quad spin device.

That is not to say that no high speed CD-ROM software packages exist, because they do. Look for more and more titles to require a quad-speed CD-ROM drive. A quad spin device is the minimum we'd recommend for new CD-ROM player purchases today, because we expect that most new software will require quad speeds or better by the end of 1996.

Sound: What Puts the Multi in Multimedia?

18

In this chapter, we'll discuss problems and difficulties that you might encounter involving sound or audio.

> **Q1: I hear it, but it's not very loud. How do I make it louder?**

Open the Sound control panel. Choose Volumes from the pop-up menu at the top (Figure 18.1), then crank up the Built-in speakers volume using the slider control on the left.

If that doesn't make it loud enough, open the Sound control panel again and crank up the Alert Sound volume, too.

> **Q2: The built-in speaker is wimpy. How do I get heart-stopping sound out of my Mac? Do I need a sound card or something? What?**

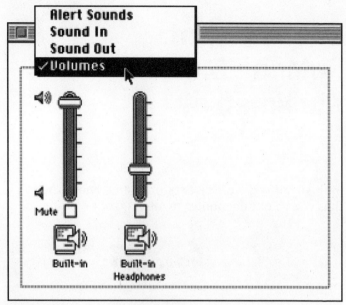

Figure 18.1 Crank up the volume using the Sound control panel.

Nope. It's a Mac. It's got excellent sound capabilities built right into it (though we admit that most Macs have a lousy speaker connected to those excellent sound capabilities).

All you need to make it louder and better are a pair of amplified speakers. Radio Shack has inexpensive ones; the major Mac mail order places have better ones. For the best sound, look for the biggest amplifier, and a sub-woofer.

Bob really likes his relatively expensive (about $300) Altec-Lansing multimedia speaker system with sub-woofer. They're real loud and have killer bass response. But you can get almost-great sound from less expensive systems.

Once you buy a speaker system, all you have to do is connect it to the sound port on the back of your Mac. One little plug. That's it.

Depending on which Macintosh model and System software version you're using, you may have to open the Sound control panel and check the Mute checkbox to turn off your Mac's internal speaker before you hear sound from your new external speakers.

Q3: I don't hear anything now that I've plugged in my fancy new multimedia amplified speakers.

Make sure they're turned on. Amplified speakers require either AC power or battery power. Also, make sure the volume is turned up on the speakers themselves.

Q4: How do I play a music CD on my CD-ROM drive?

Easy! The AppleCD Audio Player is part of your System software—there's nothing else to buy!

Just insert the disc, then choose the AppleCD Audio Player from the Apple menu and click the Play button as shown in Figure 18.2.

You can type in the song titles and disc name if you like, as we've done in Figure 18.2, but that's strictly optional.

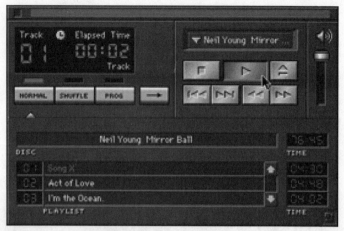

Figure 18.2 Playing an audio CD is easy; insert it and click the Play button as shown.

> **Q5: I'm trying to play a music CD. I've inserted the disc, opened the AppleCD Audio Player, and clicked the Play button. The elapsed time number changes but I don't hear anything.**

If you have an internal CD-ROM drive, try this: Open the Sound control panel. Choose Sound In from the pop-up menu (it says Alert Sounds). Click Options. Select Internal CD and Play Through. Close the Sound control panel.

If that doesn't do it, try everything in Question 3. If that's not it, see question 2. If that's not it, make sure the Mute checkbox isn't checked (if you're using the Mac's internal speaker) or that it is checked (if you're using external speakers). If you're using external speakers, make sure the plug is inserted securely into the sound port on the back of your Mac.

Q6: The sounds that come out of my speakers are crackly and distorted. What can I do?

First, check your connections outside the computer. Unplug and reconnect all of the wires that plug into speakers and the back of the Mac. Look for damaged wires or bent connections. Check the connectors and make sure they're clean and straight, too.

Second, turn the volume on your speakers down, and the volume in the Sound control panel up, and vice-versa. One element in your sound hardware chain may be overpowering the next element in the chain (like the amplifier in your Mac overpowering the amplifier in your external speakers). Experiment with different volume levels on both your speakers and the Sound control panel.

Third, check your speakers using a radio or a WalkMan. The speakers may be damaged; these symptoms can occur if you've pushed your speakers hard enough to damage their paper cones.

Before you return your speakers, it would probably be a good idea to unplug them and see if sound coming out of your Macs internal speaker is crackly and distorted. If so, your Mac may need repair; if not, take the external speakers back to the manufacturer or vendor, and exchange them. Manufacturing defects do occur and you may be the beneficiary.

Video &
QuickTime:
Makin' Movies
Work Better

19

In this chapter, we'll discuss problems and difficulties you may encounter with video, monitors, and QuickTime, the Apple System software (extension) that makes movies play on your Mac.

Q1: My screen flickers, or my system freezes. What should I do?

First re-seat all connections and power cables. Turn everything off, then jiggle all the cables and connectors. Then, restart your computer.

See the section on magnetic interference in question 2. It can cause screen flicker as well as poor picture quality.

Q2: What can I do about poor picture quality?

Try the suggestion in question 1 above, making certain all connections are solid and tight.

Clean your monitor's glass surface with a glass cleaner and a soft cloth.

Magnetic interference can reduce picture quality. This can occur when a video cable or monitor is located near metal or a strong power source. Such interference can be countered by placing special rings, called ferrite cores, around each end of the cable, one near the card and another near the monitor (these rings are available at most computer stores).

If your video cable has already been treated with ferrite rings, try re-arranging your computer's layout to re-route your video cable. Keep it as far away from speakers, power supplies, or other devices as you can.

Consult your monitor manual about proper settings for your monitor—these include: contrast, brightness, geometry, color, etc.

Change your display's resolution. Most software packages are designed for a 640x480 pixel screen. If you're using a different resolution 832x624, 800x600, 1024x768, or 1280x1024, try another setting and see if that helps.

To do this, first open the Monitors control panel, then hold down the Option key on your keyboard and click the Options button in the Monitors control panel. If your video card and monitor support alternate resolutions they'll be listed here (see Figure 19.1). Try them all to find the one best suited to the title you're using. Changes take place when you close the Monitors control panel (be sure to click the Rearrange on Close button) so it's pretty easy to try several settings.

Change your display's color depth. Most software packages are designed for 256-color displays. If you're using thousands or million of colors, reduce the color depth (again, using the Monitors control panel) and try the software again.

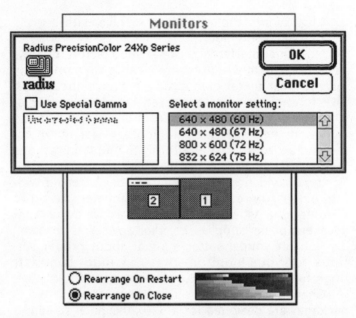

Figure 19.1 Hold down the Option key on your keyboard and click the Option button in the Monitors control panel. If your system supports alternate monitor settings, you'll see them here.

Q3: The software runs, but my videos skip, stutter, pause or have jerky sound. How can I fix this?

If the software functions properly, except for video portions, this usually indicates that your system isn't fast or powerful enough to play all the video frames at the same speed as the audio. QuickTime is dropping frames to keep pace with the sound. The following may be of help:

1. Some games offer options to vary the parameters for video and audio playback. Consult your software manual to locate the option menu or preferences dialog box. Try one of the following options, if available:

   - Reduce the number of frames per second displayed.

   - Select skip frames if behind.

   - Reduce the number of audio channels.

   - Turn off either effects, voice or music sound.

   - Decrease the size of the video window.

   - Reduce the color depth.

   - Copy the multimedia application from the CD-ROM to your hard disk (it's faster than reading from your CD-ROM, but can require significant amounts of available disk space; see the Memory chapter for details).

   - Increase or decrease the RAM used for the application (see the Memory chapter for details).

   - Keep a log of your attempts to fix the problems, and note the results. Restore settings to original values when changes don't help, or don't make a noticeable difference.

2. You may have an outdated copy of the QuickTime extension. Many games install a version of QuickTime when you run their installer; be careful only to install a newer version. In other words, don't replace a newer version with an older one, or you may make

things worse instead of better! You want version 2.0 or greater.

Note: *To check to see if your version is 2.0 or greater, click once on the QuickTime icon in your Extensions folder, then choose Get Info (shortcut: Command-I) from the File menu). If its version number is below 2.0, find a copy of QuickTime 2.0 or greater (many games install it when you run their installers; it's also available directly from Apple) and replace the older version with the new one.*

3. Virtual Memory or RamDoubler. If Virtual Memory is turned on in the Memory control panel or you're using Connectix' RamDoubler, you may experience choppy movie playback. Turn Virtual Memory off in the Memory control panel or remove/disable RamDoubler, then restart. (For a more detailed explanation, see the next chapter, Memory: Things to Remember.)

4. Buy a faster Mac.

Memory: Things to Remember

20

In this chapter we'll look at RAM—Random Access Memory—the expensive silicon chips we never seem to have enough of, and how to get the most out of however little you have.

> **Q1: I only have 4 (or 5) megabytes of RAM. I can't play most games without Virtual Memory or RamDoubler. But you said they may cause QuickTime movies to play back poorly.**

It's even worse than if you use either Virtual Memory or RamDoubler. Overall performance of many CD-ROM titles, not just ones that have QuickTime movies, will suffer. The bottom line is that you need at least 8Mb of RAM to run many of today's multimedia titles. And as time passes, fewer and fewer titles will run on 4 or 5 meg machines. So the best answer is, upgrade to 8 or more megs of RAM if you can possibly afford it.

No matter how much or how little RAM you have, for best results and highest performance turn Virtual Memory off in the Memory control panel or remove/disable RamDoubler, then restart.

And see Chapter 16 for tips on how to disable unneeded extensions and control panels, which leave more RAM available for your multimedia programs.

> **Q2: I've disabled all unnecessary extensions and control panels and I still get a "not enough memory" error when I try to launch the game.**

The Disk Cache, which you adjust using the Memory control panel, can use up RAM. The Disk Cache automatically stores frequently used data from your hard disk in RAM. While this theoretically speeds up your Mac, it also means the RAM used by the cache isn't available to your multimedia program. Here's the fix:

Open your Memory control panel and use the little arrows to lower the Disk Cache setting to its lowest number, 32K. Close the Memory control panel and restart (see Figure 20.1).

If you don't believe this works, open About This Macintosh before you make the adjustment. Note the Largest Unused Block size. Now adjust the Disk Cache and restart. Now look at About This Macintosh again. The Largest Unused Block should have grown

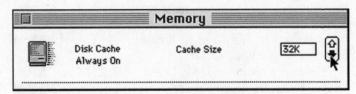

Figure 20.1 Lowering the Disk Cache to 32K leaves more RAM available for multimedia programs.

about the same amount as the Disk Cache was before you adjusted it.

One last thing: If your Mac has 8 or fewer megabytes of RAM, you might want to leave your Disk Cache set to 32K all the time to allow more memory for programs to run in. However, if you do, you may notice a slight slowdown. If so, try increasing the Disk Cache slightly (but remember that every K of RAM the Disk Cache uses is a K of RAM your programs CAN'T use).

> **Q3: I've got lots of RAM—16 (or more) megs of it. Can I use any of it to make my multimedia titles run faster?**

Maybe. See the previous question about the Disk Cache. Increasing its size may provide some speed improvement. Again, don't forget: memory (RAM) used by the Disk Cache isn't available to programs. If you set it too high, you won't have enough memory to run your multimedia applications.

Getting the most out of the Disk Cache takes a bit of trial and error. Try increasing it 32K or 64K at a time, then restarting and trying your multimedia program again. If you don't notice an increase in speed, increase it some more and restart again. If you don't notice an increase in speed even at high settings, just change it back to 32K and forget about it. (Some people are more sensitive to the speed changes than others.)

Another way to (perhaps) make your multimedia title run faster is to allocate more RAM to it. You can only do this if the program is installed on your hard disk. (In other words, you can't adjust memory allocations for applications which reside on a CD-ROM disc;

see Question 5 if your title runs directly from the CD and didn't install itself on your hard disk automatically).

Here's how: First, find out how much free memory is available on your Mac. Quit all open applications except the Finder and then look at About This Macintosh. The Largest Unused Block represents the amount of RAM available for your program or programs. Write this number down. (It was 7,443 in Figure 16.1, remember?)

Next, single click on the multimedia application on your hard disk and Get Info (choose Get Info from the File menu or use the shortcut Command-I). This brings up the Info window for the multimedia program (see Figure 20.2). Select the number in the Preferred size box and type in a new one. Remember you only have so much RAM available (the number you wrote down in the previous step). Also remember that it's a good idea to leave several hundred K of RAM free for your Mac. So type a number 200-300K lower than the Largest Unused Block.

Close the Info window and launch the program (no need to restart your Mac this time). Many programs run faster when they've been given a larger Preferred size.

Q4: I've increased the Preferred memory size. Now when I launch the program I receive a not enough memory error.

You didn't allow enough free memory for your Mac itself. Repeat the steps in the previous question, and type in a Preferred memory size slightly lower than before. Try again. If it doesn't work, lower the Preferred memory setting a little more. Repeat as necessary.

```
┌──────────────────────────────────────────────────┐
│ ■□ ══════════ Vortex Info ══════════             │
├──────────────────────────────────────────────────┤
│                                                    │
│    🌀    Vortex                                   │
│                                                    │
│    Kind : application program                      │
│    Size : 2 MB on disk (2,182,836 bytes           │
│           used)                                    │
│   Where : The Rest of It : CD ROM Lg Installs :    │
│           The Vortex :                             │
│                                                    │
│  Created : 6/8/95, 2:28 PM                          │
│ Modified : 7/8/95, 6:29 PM                          │
│  Version : 1.0.0 © Copyright HyperBole              │
│            Studios, 1995                            │
│ Comments :                                         │
│  ┌──────────────────────────────────────────────┐ │
│  │                                                │ │
│  │                                                │ │
│  └──────────────────────────────────────────────┘ │
│             ┌····Memory Requirements·····┐         │
│             : Suggested size :   4300    K :       │
│             :                              :       │
│             : Minimum size : [ 4300 ]    K :       │
│  □ Locked   :                              :       │
│             : Preferred size : [ 7200 ]  K :       │
│             └····························· ┘         │
└──────────────────────────────────────────────────┘
```

Figure 20.2 Many multimedia programs run faster when you increase their Preferred memory size as shown here.

Q5: I can't type anything into the Preferred size box!

You're trying to adjust the memory size of an application stored on a CD-ROM disk. Since a CD-ROM disk is read only, it won't let you adjust the Preferred size of items that are stored on it.

If the CD has an Installer, run it, then try the procedure on the copy of the software it installs on your hard disk.

If the CD doesn't have an Installer, you may not be out of luck yet. Try copying the main application icon from the CD to your hard disk if you have room on your hard disk for it. Or, if the application is in a folder on the CD-ROM, copy the entire folder to your hard disk if you have room. (Don't forget: Get Info tells you the size of the file or folder!) Once you have a copy on your hard disk, try adjusting its Preferred size.

Note that this technique doesn't work with all multimedia titles—some of them MUST be run directly from the CD-ROM. If yours is one of them and you still get "not enough memory" errors after disabling extensions and control panels and reducing Disk Cache, you don't have enough memory for that title. You could try running it with Virtual Memory enabled (in the Memory control panel), but that will probably cause degraded performance. Still, if you're determined to run the title, it may be your only hope short of a RAM upgrade.

> **Q6: I don't see any of the memory things in the Info window.**

You've selected something other than the multimedia application—a disk icon, folder icon, or the icon of one of the titles support files. Only applications can have their memory allocations adjusted. Select a different icon and Get Info on it instead.

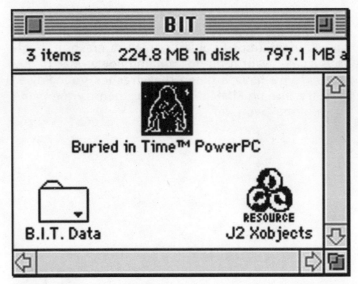

Figure 20.3 The application icon is at the top (Buried in Time PowerPC) of the BIT folders window. Its preferred memory allocation can be adjusted using the Get Info box. The icons below it are for support files (B.I.T. Data and J2 Xobjects); their memory allocations cannot be adjusted.

Only the application itself will have a Memory Requirements box at the bottom of its Info window; other files (documents, folders, and disk icons, for example) don't have fields for adjusting memory.

You can usually tell which one is the multimedia application by its name (often the same as what's on the game box). Also, the application icon is usually at the top of the window when you open the games folder, with support files and folders below it (see Figure 20.3).

Q7: I have a Power Macintosh. Anything special I should know about memory?

183

Be mindful of Modern Memory Manager. This option, in the Memory control panel, if it's turned on, causes many (mostly older) games to crash. Though you usually want it on, for running Power Mac native stuff, if you have a game that crashes your Power Mac, try turning MMM off. Restart, then try the game again. It may work now.

The Final Word: A Few More Tips, Hints, and Troubleshooting Suggestions

21

In this chapter we'll cover the last few things that haven't been covered in previous chapters. After this, you should know enough to solve just about any CD-ROM related problem on your Macintosh.

> **Q1: The program crashes (freezes, bombs, quits unexpectedly, etc.) when I launch it. What is happening?**

There are several things it could be. The program you're trying to launch could have a conflict with an extension or control panel. Try disabling all but those necessary for using a CD-ROM (see Chapter 16).

If you used an Installer: one of the files it installed may be defective. Get rid of it by dragging it (or the folder it's in, if it's in a folder on your hard disk) to the Trash and choosing Empty Trash from the Special menu. Then reinstall and try again. If you have a Power Mac and the installer offers a Native PowerPC option, choose it.

If the program is poorly written it could be crashing impolitely due to lack of RAM. Make sure the program's Preferred memory size (in its Get Info window) is several hundred K lower than the Largest Unused Block (in the About This Macintosh window). See Chapters 16 and 20 for details.

Finally, check your Monitors control panel and set it to the proper number of colors for the title you're trying to use. Most (but not all) games run at 256 colors. When you launch most modern games, they either switch your Mac to the proper number of colors automatically (and then set it back the way it was when you quit), or display a dialog box asking permission to switch your Mac to the proper number of colors. Some games aren't this smart. If you don't set your monitor to the proper number of colors, they refuse to start up. Look in the manual or Read Me file for the recommended monitor setting, set it in Monitors control panel, and try again.

> **Q2: I have a quad-speed CD-ROM drive and it still seems slow to me. Anything I can do besides buy a faster drive?**

Well, there are some things that might help. One such thing is called a caching driver. Your Mac needs to be running special software that lets it read CD-ROM discs. That software is called the CD-ROM driver software. The Apple CD-ROM extension is yours. You got it free with your Mac (or paid for with your Macintosh System Software upgrade).

Apple CD-ROM works, but it's not tuned for high-performance. A caching driver, such as FWBs CD-ROM Toolkit or CharisMacs CD AutoCache, can make your CD-ROM drive seem to run faster. They're both very good. After installing either, many of your CD-ROM titles will run noticeably faster, almost like magic. For well under $100, they're a good investment if you spend a lot of time using your CD-ROM drive.

Two other things that can make your drive feel sluggish are:

1. Another program running in the background. *Solution:* Choose all open programs from the Application menu in the upper-right corner, then Quit (Command-Q) them.

2. Loading unneeded extensions or control panels at startup. *Solution:* Disable all extensions and control panels except the ones your Mac needs for CD-ROMs (see Chapter 16).

Q3: Any other inexpensive ways to soup up my Mac for multimedia?

As mentioned previously, Macs have marvelous sound capabilities. A good pair of amplified speakers makes most CD-ROM titles much more enjoyable.

Another thing that makes life easier is an extension manager, so you can turn extensions and control panels on and off easily (see Chapter 16). If you buy a System 7.5 upgrade (or your Mac came with System 7.5 installed on it), you'll get Extensions Manager. This is the recommended solution. System 7.5 also includes lots of other goodies like the latest version of QuickTime and the Sound control panel, and lots of other fixes and tweaks that make your Mac better.

If for some reason you don't want to upgrade to System 7.5, there are very good extension managers available from Now Software and Casady & Greene for well under $100.

Q4: How come there are so many pages about DOS and Windows and so few pages devoted to the Mac?

It's because a CD-ROM title is much more likely to work the first time you try it on a Mac. Most of the tech support people we talked to said the same thing —they get many more calls for support from people with Windows machines than from people with Macs. It's that simple!

That's why there are a lot more pages of problems that relate to the PC and Windows. Just look at some of the chapters they have to have and we don't. For example, the Mac section has no modem chapter because we couldn't find any modem-linked games for the Mac that were on CD-ROM. And the few network games we found (only a couple come on CD-ROM) seemed to work fine, as long as our network— LocalTalk or Ethernet—was wired up properly. So the Mac section has no network chapter, either. A special software chapter? Nah. We don't need additional software (other than the couple of items mentioned earlier in this chapter). A Windows chapter? No way. Keyboards, Joysticks, and Mice? With the Mac, just plug em in and play away. The Mac offers plug and play convenience that Windows (and Windows 95) can't touch. As we said at the beginning of this sec-tion—you made the right choice of computer for mul-timedia!

The bottom line is we've covered everything we can think of that could go wrong with your Mac and CD-ROM drive. It just took us a lot fewer pages to do it for the Mac than it did for the PC.

If you've read all the Mac chapters and still can't make it work, it's time to throw in the towel and call the manufacturer. If it's a specific disc that's the problem, call its publisher; if you can't get the CD-ROM drive to work, call Apple (1-800-SOS-APPL) or the manufacturer of your CD-ROM drive. Good luck!

Appendix A

CD-ROM Glossary

("Jeopardy style"—with the answer in the form of a question.)

16 bit How do you describe a monitor or video card capable of displaying thousands of colors at once (65536 colors, to be precise)?

24 bit How do you describe a monitor or video card capable of displaying millions of colors at once (16 million, give or take a few)?

8 bit How do you describe a monitor or video card capable of displaying 256 colors at once?

16550 UART chip What is the high speed data flow device on a serial port that allows up to 115,000 bps transfer rate?

About This Macintosh (Mac only) Where do you look to find out what version of the System software you're running, how much RAM is installed in your Mac, and how much RAM is available for multimedia titles? (Hint: You find it under the Apple menu in the Finder)

Apple CD-ROM extension (Mac only) Name one of the extensions that must be in your Extensions folder at startup for your CD-ROM drive to work properly?

Apple Photo Access extension (Mac only) Which extension must be in your Extensions folder at startup for your CD-ROM drive to be able to read PhotoCD formatted CDs?

AppleCD Audio Player desk accessory (Mac only) Name the desk accessory you use to play Audio CDs on your Mac CD-ROM drive? (Hint: You find it under the Apple menu in the Finder)

AUTOEXEC.BAT (PC only) What do you get when you cross Lee Iacocca with a vampire? (Also: What is the name of the file containing the BATch of instructions your PC EXECutes AUTOmatically when it starts up?)

available disk space What do you call the space on your hard disk that's not already taken up by stuff?

AVI What is Audio Video Interleaved? Or, what is one of the standard video compression formats designed for use with Windows' Media Player application?

backup What will you be sorry for if you don't do? Or, what is the act of protecting your data by making additional copies of your files?

base memory What is another name for conventional memory? Or, what is the first 640K of memory on a PC where all software executions must occur?

baud rate What is the unit of measure commonly used to describe how fast a modem transmits and receives data?

BIOS (PC only) What is a set of instructions, usually on a chip inside your computer, that tells it how to communicate with peripherals, disk drives, and other equipment? Or, what is the F.L.A. (Four Letter Acronym) for Basic Input/Output System?

boot disk   **PC:** What do you call the disk, floppy or hard, the PC starts up from? **Mac:** What do you call the disk, floppy or hard, the Mac starts up from?

buffer What is the term used to describe the area of memory used on a CD-ROM to temporarily store data before it gets transferred to the CPU? Or, what is the term that should be used on the packaging of a CD-ROM drive instead of cache?

bus slot (PC only) What is the long slender edge connector on a motherboard designed to connect an expansion card?

cache What do you call a place in memory (RAM) where the computer can temporarily store data for faster access?

caddy What do you call the plastic deal that protects a CD-ROM disc, required for some CD-ROM drives.
Bonus answer: Caddyless (or tray-loading) CD-ROM drives.
Bonus question: Which type of CD-ROM drive do Ed and Bob prefer?)

CD disc (a.k.a. audio CD disc) What are discs that look like CD-ROM discs but have music on them called?

CD-ROM What are discs that look like plain old music CDs but instead contain cool multimedia stuff to play on your computer called?

CD-ROM driver   PC: What is the software which gives your system the instructions to control a CD-ROM device?   **Mac:** What do you call the piece of software your Mac needs in order to use CD-ROM discs? If you have an Apple CD-ROM drive, What is Apple CD-ROM is also an acceptable answer.

CIF (Computer Information File) What is the collection of all relevant information about your computer system, its components, and their overall configuration? See Chapter 1?

clean boot What is the term used to describe booting a computer while loading the minimum number of drivers to enable only the basic system operations, which is often accomplished by using a boot disk?

clock speed What is the rate at which a CPU operates, usually measured in MHz (1024K Hertz, or cycles per second)?

clone What do you call a computer that looks, acts, and performs as well as or better, and costs less than a similar model from IBM or Apple?

color depth (see 8 bit, 16 bit, 24 bit)

comm port What is another term used to refer to a serial port?

command strings What are the series of letters and numbers used to change the settings and operation of a modem?

compatibility What is it called when your existing hardware and/or software get along perfectly with your new hardware and/or software?

compressed air What is the stuff, somehow squashed into a spray can, used to blow crud out of your computer or CD-ROM drive?

compression What do you call smooshing a file, usually a video or other multimedia file, to make it smaller so more files can fit on the disc?

CompuServe   What is the name of the largest commercial on-line service, with the most files and conferences, at the time this book was published?

CONFIG.SYS   What is the file used by DOS to specify device drivers, buffers, and lots of other arcane stuff used to establish a SYStem CONFIGuration?

Control Panel   PC: What is the application in Windows where the user can add or remove drivers, change system parameters and vary environmental settings?   **Mac:** What is a utility that lets you modify the behavior of a hardware attribute such as mouse, keyboard, monitor, etc.?

conventional memory   What is the 640K area of memory that all software must execute within on a PC? Or, what is the standard term for base memory?

copyright   What is the legal right granted to an author, a composer, a playwright, a publisher, or a distributor to exclusive publication, production, sale, or distribution of a literary, musical, dramatic, or artistic work?

CPU   What do you call your computers main (brain?) chip? Or, what is an acronym for Central Processing Unit?

crash (also bomb, freeze, unexpectedly quit, GPF, etc.)   What do you call it when your computer stops working properly due to hardware or software problems?

default   What is another word for the way it will be unless you change it? Or, what is the state or condition your computer assumes unless you tell it otherwise?

DEFRAG.EXE   What is the DOS 5.0 (and higher) tool which will defragment a hard drive?

defragment   What is the process which rearranges fragmented files on a hard drive so that each file occupies contiguous clusters, thus improving access and transfer rates?

diagnostic   What is the process of retrieving information about a system?

DIP switches   What are those barbaric little Dual In-Line

Pin switches often used for setting ID numbers on internal and/or SCSI devices?

directory tree What is a listing of the directories and possible files on a hard drive in a recrusive format? Or, what is a hierarchical listing of all the directories and files on a disk drive called?

disc caddy (see caddy)

Disk Cache   PC: What is the adjustable area of memory (RAM) set aside for frequently-accessed information? **Mac:** What is the adjustable area of memory (RAM) set aside for frequently-accessed information? Or, what can eat up your precious RAM almost as fast as a folder full of extraneous extensions?

DMA (Direct Memory Access) What is the term used to describe the transfer of data between memory and a peripheral without intervention from the CPU?

DOS What is the T.L.A. (Three Letter Acronym) for Disk Operating System, the software at your computers heart?

DRAM (Dynamic RAM; more commonly, the type of memory (RAM) in your computer) What is something almost everyone could use more of? Or, what is a computer's short term memory called?

driver (see also CD-ROM driver) What is the software that gives a computer the instructions and abilities needed to access and control peripheral equipment or internal software?

EMM386.SYS What is the name of the memory manager which ships with DOS, which has the ability to use extended memory as expanded memory?

emulation What is the term used to describe the ability of a device or software to act like another device or software of a different brand, make or model?

environmental variables What are the controlling entities which set boundaries and define the emulation modes for a particular OS session?

Expanded memory (EMS) What is a high memory usage method which uses a page switching technique? See Chapter 4?

Extended memory (XMS) What is the high memory usage method which gives software access by enabling the protected mode of operation? See Chapter 4?

extension (Mac only) What are small programs that load at startup as long as they're in the Extensions folder?

Extensions Manager control panel (Mac only) What is the name of the nifty little program, free with System 7.5, that lets you turn your extensions and control panels on and off quickly and easily?

external (external CD-ROM drive) What do you call a device connected to your computer by a cable?

ferrite rings What are metal rings attached to the ends of a monitor cable in order to reduce interference with other electrical or magnetic sources?

file type What is the term used to describe saving information with a file extension which associates the file with a specific format of data?

Finder (Mac only) What is the name of the disk and file management program, the one that appears when the Mac first starts up, the one with the disk icon in the upper-right corner and the trash can in the lower right?

F.L.A. What is the abbreviation for the phrase defining the acronym derived from the first letters from four words.

Foreign File Access extension (Mac only) What is another file that must be in the Extensions folder for your Mac and CD-ROM drive to work properly?

Freeware What do you call freely distributable software, for which there is no charge?

game port The term used to refer to the adapter connector where a joystick is attached to a computer system?

GPF What is the label given to thousands of errors which occur under Windows which gives little or no explanation to the actual origin or cause of the error?

High Memory Areas (HMA) What is the area of RAM above 1M?

High Sierra File Access extension (Mac only) What is yet another file that must be in the Extensions folder for your Mac and CD-ROM drive to work properly?

HIMEM.SYS What is the upper memory manager that ships with DOS?

I/O addr What is a synonym for trials and tribulations when configuring a PC? Or, what is the starting memory address for the memory buffers used to transfer information to and from a PC peripheral device?

IDE What is the standard type of hard drive on a PC? Or, what is an acronym for Integrated Drive Electronics?

install What is the term used to describe the process of adding a software or hardware product to a computer system?

installer What do you call the program that places all the software necessary to use a CD-ROM disc on your hard disk?

interface What is the term used to describe the method or mechanism of communication between a computer and its user?

internal What do you call any device: hard drive, CD-ROM drive, modem, etc. that lives inside your computer case?

Internet What is the proper name for the giant, multinational network of connected computers, sometimes referred to as the information superhighway?

IRQ (Interrupt ReQuest) What is a special CPU handle that allows the processor to halt normal instruction execution and handle input or output to a computer peripheral device on demand?

ISO 9660 File Access extension (Mac only) What is yet another file that must be in the Extensions folder for your Mac and CD-ROM drive to work properly?

jumpers What do you call the small, usually plastic, usually rectangular-shaped plugs you slide on or off of little tiny pins on a circuit board? (Extra credit: add the words in order to control options for that circuit board.)

K or Kilobyte What is the term used to describe the size of computer memory or storage products in 1024 bytes?

logical drive What do you call a hard disk you can have a meaningful conversation with? Or, what is a hard disk partition that is permanantly assigned a drive letter?

M or Megabyte What is the term used to describe the size of computer memory or storage products in 1024K or 1,048,576 bytes?

math co-processor What is the name of the assisting device for a CPU which handles mathematical functions?

MEM.EXE What is the utility shipped with DOS that is useful for retrieving information about current memory size and the locations of loaded drivers, TSRs and other software?

MEMMAKER.EXE What is the utility shipped with DOS that can optimize the start up files to increase available conventional memory?

Memory control panel (Mac only) What do you call the little program that allows you to adjust the disk cache, virtual memory, RAM disk, and Modern Memory Manager or 32-bit addressing?

memory manager What is the general name of utilities which can manipulate memory areas below and/or above 1M?

MHz What is the frequency used to measure the clock speed of a CPU?

Microsoft Mouse What is the name of the industry-standard rodent-like pointing device?

MIDI What is the F.L.A. (Four Letter Acronym) for Musical Instrument Digital Interface, a standard for encoding and decoding sound for use with a computer?

minimum requirements What must the least-powerful computer configuration capable of running a CD-ROM title meet or exceed?

modem What is a device that allows data, text, video, sound, anything to be sent from one computer to another over plain old telephone lines?

monitor What is the part of your computer that looks like a television set?

Monitors control panel (Mac only) What is the small program used to control the number of colors your monitor displays?

motherboard What is the name of the large resin board where the CPU, memory modules and bus slots are located?

MOUSE.COM What is the name of the standard Microsoft driver for a mouse?

MOV What is the extension name of the video compression type known by its full name of QuickTime Video? Extra credit: What is the file type for QuickTime MOVies?

MPC Level What is the name of the minimum system requirements (CPU, RAM, display, disk size, etc.) for a multimedia PC?

MPG or MPEG What is the name of a video compression method developed by the Motion Picture Experts Group?

MSCDEX.EXE What is the name of the DOS utility that provides DOS with hard drive-like access to a CD-ROM device?

MSD.EXE What is the DOS utility that is useful for obtaining information about a PC's system and configuration? Or, what is the utility filename for the Microsoft Diagnostics program?

Non-Interlaced What is the term used to describe the method of refreshing a monitor screen line by line, flicker free?

parallel port What do you call the plug receptacle on the back of your computer, the one you use to connect parallel devices, usually printers?

parameter What is the term used to describe information included after a program call that defines boundaries, options or variable settings for proper or preferred execution?

patch What is the term used to describe a fix to an errant software product?

PCI What is a bus type which allows 32- or 64-bit communications between an expansion card and a PC's CPU?

peripheral What do you call devices like hard drives, CD-ROM drives, printers, modems, etc. that you connect to your computer?

pre-load What is the term used to describe the practice of loading a driver before executing a program? Or, what is the term used to describe the practice of installing and configuring software on a computer system prior to sale?

preferred memory size (Mac only) What is the amount of memory a program uses? (Assuming, that is, that much memory is available; you could check it by looking at the Largest Unused Block number in About This Macintosh.)

processor (see CPU)

proprietary What do you call technology that belongs to one and only one company? (You have to buy Zip cartridges from their inventor, Iomega. Nobody else is allowed to make Zip cartridges. The Zip technology is proprietary.)

Qsound What is a new technology of making sounds three-dimension, so that missiles sound as if they are coming from any direction?

QuickTime What do you call the technology from Apple Computer, Inc., that lets you play and record movies on any computer running the Mac Operating System?

QuickTime extension (Mac only) What do you call the extension (which must be in the Extensions folder at startup to load) that lets you play and record movies?

RAM What is the T.L.A. for Random Access Memory? Or, what do you call a computer's short-term memory (and also the memory chips themselves)?

RamDoubler What do you call a program (Extension, actually) that makes your computer act as though it has twice as much memory as it actually has?

random access memory (see RAM)

REM What is the command term used in batch files, like startup and INI files, to prevent a command from being executed without removing it from the file?

resolution What do you call the number of pixels per inch your monitor displays?

restart   PC: What is the method of hitting the reset switch or momentarily turning off the power in order to reboota PC?   **Mac:** What is it called when you choose Restart from the Finders Special menu, causing your Mac to shut down momentarily, then start back up?

Return Merchandise Authorization (RMA) What is the number required by many shipping departments in order to send a product back for reimbursement or repair?

SCSI What is the F.L.A. for Small Computer System Interface, a standard for connecting high-speed devices such as hard disks, CD-ROM drives, and scanners to Macs or PCs?

SCSI ID number Each SCSI device in the SCSI chain must have a unique one of what?

SCSI termination What must the last device in the SCSI chain have (at least, a chain of two or more devices)?

seek time What is the term used to describe the length of time required by a storage device to find a specified bit of information?

serial port What do you call the connection on the back of your computer where you plug in serial devices such as mice, modems and printers?

shareware What do you call software that is free to try, but if you like it and continue to use it, you're honor-bound to send the author a specified fee?

SmartDrive What is the DOS caching utility that has the ability to cache CD-ROM drives since DOS version 6.2?

Sound Blaster What do you call the most popular brand of PC sound card?

Sound control panel (Mac) What do you call the little program (it lives in the Control Panels folder) that you use to adjust volume levels and enable external speakers?

stereo What do you call two-channel sound?

SVGA What is the standard for monitors which required a minimum of 800x600 pixels at 4 bits per pixel (or allows each pixel to be 1 of 16 colors)?

System 6.X (Mac only) What do you call a creaky old version of the Macintosh Operating System?

System 7 (System 7.X, System 7.5, etc.) (Mac only) What do you call the current generation of the Macintosh Operating System?

system freeze or system lock or lock-up What is it called when, due to hardware or software failure, your mouse and keyboard go dead and your only option is to flick off the power switch?

SYSTEM.INI What is one of the significant startup initialization files for Windows where devices and system parameters are set?

third-party What is the term used to describe a product that was created by an outside company?

transfer rate What is the term used to describe the speed at which data is transferred between a storage device and the CPU?

TSR What is the name of software that remains in memory after it has executed and/or waits in memory to be called to re-execute? Or, what is the acronym for Terminate-and-Stay-Resident?

UNDELETE.EXE What is the DOS utility that enables you to retrieve recently deleted files whose data remains on the disk in good condition?

uninstall What is the term used to describe a method for removing a software or hardware product from a computer system, so that no trace of its previous existence remains?

Upper Memory Blocks (UMB) What is the area of memory between 640K and 1M often used for BIOS and device drivers, and which is controlled by the DOS utility HIMEM.SYS?

VESA BIOS Extension What is the term used to describe a standard video control interface defined the Video Electronics Standards Association?

video mode What is the term used to describe the possible states for monitors and video cards, that vary in color depth, pixel width and refresh rate?

Views control panel (Mac only) What do you call the small program you use to turn on "show disk info in header" so you know how much unused space remains on your hard disk?

Virtual Memory   PC: Under Windows, what is the use of hard drive space as a slow extension to system RAM?

Mac: What do you call the scheme, built into the System Software, that lets you substitute unused hard disk space for RAM, albeit with limited success?

VLB What is a bus type which allows 32-bit communication between an expansion card and the CPU? Or, what is the acronym for Video Local Bus?

VRAM What is the F.L.A. for Video Random Access Memory? Or, what is a fast and efficient memory technology for transferring data between a video adapter and a PC's CPU?

WAV What is the sound file type most commonly used in Windows?

wavetable What is the name for the collection of samples of real instruments used by a sound card to recreate a realistic sound of that instrument?

WebCrawler— http://webcrawler.cs.washington.edu/WebCrawler/ What is a great search utility on the Internet's World Wide Web?

WinCIM What is the Windows platform CompuServe interface?

WIN.INI What is one of the significant startup initialization files for Windows where devices and system parameters are set?

Windows What is the popular graphical operating system/environment installed over DOS on a PC which was created by the eminent tycoon, Bill Gates?

Yahoo—http://www.yahoo.com/ What is the best searchable database of World Wide Web sites on the Internet?

Appendix B

Summary of Questions

Chapter 1: Questions to Ask Before Problems Occur

Q1: The setup asks for information about my computer, like memory size, CPU speed, COM ports, etc. Where can I find this information?

Q2: I ran out of disk space during the installation. What can I do about it?

Q3: The software says I have an incompatible product installed on my computer, or that I'm lacking a specific required product. How can I be sure?

Q4: What are "minimum requirements?"

Q5: I updated my software, and my old configuration, setup or data files are gone. What happened?

Q6: I started to install new software but it crashed during installation, or I aborted during installation, or it finished installing, and now my computer doesn't work the way it did before. What can I do now?

Q7: Where are my backups? & Where is my CIF?

Chapter 2: CD-ROM Drives—Compact Disc or Chaos Director?

Q1: It worked before but it doesn't work now. What can I do?

Q2: I can't read the disc directory, I can't run any of

the programs on the disc, or the CD-ROM drive does not appear in the File Manager or as a DOS device. What should I do?

Q3: The drive doesn't appear to work. What can I do?

Q4: I just changed discs, why do I still see the directory for the previous disc?

Q5: My CD has dirt, finger prints or dust on the data surface. How should I clean it?

Q6: AARRGGHH! My disc has scratches, is there any hope?

Q7: My CD-ROM seems to read discs poorly. Can I fix this?

Q8: What is an MPC level?

Q9: What is a cache, and can I use one with my CD-ROM?

Q10: What is a buffer and how is it used?

Q11: I bought a new Quad or Hex spin CD-ROM drive, but my programs don't seem to run any faster. Why?

Chapter 3: Sound

DOS:

Q1: When I run my game, or its set up utility, my PC locks up. Why does it do this?

Q2: I've reconfigured my sound card and checked it against the rest of my computer hardware, but my game still locks up. What now?

Q3: My game runs fine, but I don't hear any sound at all, or I only hear sound effects, or I only hear music, or I can't hear any digitized voices. How can I get all the sound I'm supposed to?

Q4: My game runs OK, but the sound is jerky. Why does it start and stop while it's playing?

Q5: The sounds that come out of my speakers are crackly and distorted. What can I do?

Q6: When I installed my sound card's software it changed my AUTOEXEC.BAT and my CONFIG.SYS. I was told never to mess with these. What should I do?

Q6: The setup utility for the sound card asks for an IRQ, an I/O address, the MIDI port address and DMA settings for my sound card. How do I scope these out?

Windows:

WQ1: I can't get Windows to make any sounds. Why not?

WQ2: When my system plays a sound, Windows freezes or reboots. Why?

Misc:

MQ1: I have an internal CD-ROM and a sound card. I should be able to play music CDs through my computer, but I can't hear any music. Why not?

MQ2: I've covered everything mentioned in this chapter, but I still have sound problems. What else can I do?

Chapter 4: Memory—Can You Remember RAM?

Q1: When I start installing or when I try to run a program, I get an error that states that I do not have enough conventional or base memory. How can I fix this?

Q2: The software instructions for building a boot disk didn't work or I didn't understand them. How should I create a boot disk?

Q3: The software requires EMS. How do I provide it?

Q4: My software doesn't work with EMS; how can I turn it off?

Q5: I've got all the RAM required for this software but it doesn't function correctly (or work at all). What can I do?

Q6: How can I use MEMMAKER to optimize my start-up files?

Chapter 5:   Video—Can You See the Light?

Q1: Under Windows, my screen flickers, I get a GPFs, or my system freezes. What should I do?

Q2: What can I do about poor picture quality?

Q3: I just installed new software, and now Windows won't work. What can I do?

Q4: The software runs, but my videos skip, stutter, pause or have jerky sound. How can I fix this?

Q5: What is the VESA BIOS Extension?

Q6: I purchased a 17" monitor (or larger), but when I run some software the pictures are jagged and I can see individual pixels. Shouldn't a large monitor behave better than this?

Chapter 6:   Keyboards, Joysticks, and Mouses: Should We Get More Cheese?

Q1: My keyboard doesn't work, or a few keys no longer function. What can I do?

Q2: My joystick is not functioning or doesn't perform like it should. What can I do?

Q3: Eke! Why won't my mouse work?

Chapter 7:   Modems—Can You Make the Call?

Q1: My new software program cannot locate my modem, or it fails to operate the modem. What can I do?

Q2: I just faxed a document successfully, so why won't my terminal program dial?

Q3: Why won't my machine's modem connect to another modem?

Chapter 8:   ARRGGHH! Windows Broke, AGAIN!

Q1: I installed a new program; now, Windows won't work. What can I do?

Q2: Windows runs but my screen is incorrectly sized, or the color depth or resolution has changed. How can I fix this?

Q3: I just installed a software package; why won't my mouse work now?

Q4: While using a new software package, Windows has started acting strangely. Fonts change sizes, letters disappear, icons black out, applications won't load, etc. What can I do?

Chapter 9:   You Mean, I Need Other Software Too!?

Q1: What software do I need to operate my CD-ROM at its best?

Q2: What software do I need to view movies and graphics?

Q3: How can I view the graphics on a CD-ROM disc?

Q4: How can I listen to sounds from a CD-ROM?

Q5: There are a bunch of files on my CD-ROM which I cannot get any third-party application to read or understand. Is something wrong?

Chapter 10: Look Out! Some Software Hurts More Than It Helps!

Q1: The installation utility did not ask me for a target directory; instead, it added a directory and files to my C drive, but I wanted them only on the D drive. Why?

Q2: The installation utility didn't ask for permission to overwrite my previous configuration for an older version. Why not?

Q3: The installation utility added commands to my startup files without asking. The installation utility did not make backups of the startup files it changed. The installation utility did not create a log of the changes it made to my system. Why do these things happen to me?

Q4: The installation/setup utility doesn't provide an uninstall option. Why not?

Q5: The installation utility changed Windows' video mode, or some other operational driver, or my Windows INI files, or Windows no longer functions. Why did it do this to me?

Q6: The installation utility added a group window under Program Manager without asking. The installation utility did not ask which group to add the new icons to. Why?

Q7: The software requires me to re-configure my sound/video/SCSI/etc. card back to the factory default, but all my other software and hardware works fine with the current configuration. What should I do?

Q8: The software did things that the documentation left out, or that it didn't explain completely. Why?

Chapter 11:   Speed and Optimization—How Fast Is Fast Enough?

Q1: How can I get my CD-ROM to work faster?

Q2: How can I improve my system's performance?

Chapter 12:   Tech Support: They Are There to Help, Right?!

Q1: How do I know that I have a real problem?

Q2: What should I do before calling tech support?

Q3: What do I need to know before calling tech support?

Q4: What do I do as I get ready to call?

Q5: When's the best time to call tech support?

Q6: I finally got through to a real person, what should I do?

Q7: What do I do after the call?

Q8: What do I do with the solution?

Q9: What if I can't get through to a human?

Q10: I don't want to get stuck in "hold hell" waiting for a technician on the phone. Are there other ways to get technical support without waiting forever?

Chapter 13:   RDA—RecommendeD minimum configurAtion

Q1: What's a good PC system configuration for running multimedia and CD-ROM based software?

Q2: What is a good software base upon which to configure a multimedia environment?

Chapter 14:   Drop the Dead Donkey!

Q1: What were the authors' basic assumptions?

Q2: What software version assumptions did we make?

Q3: Did you assume we could edit a file?

Q4: Did you assume we knew how to make a backup, and restore data from backups?

Q5: Did you assume we would read the glossary?

Q6: Did you assume we would read Chapter 1?

Chapter 15:   The Windows 95 Experience

Q1: What can I do to optimize the use of my CD-ROM in Win 95?

Q2: I have an IDE CD-ROM drive or another non-standard interface CD-ROM drive which does not seem to work with Win 95. What can I do?

Q3: I retrieved a new driver to allow my old hardware to work under Win 95. How can I install this driver?

Q4: How can I install a new software package on Windows 95?

Q5: What is the best place to get help or other information about Windows 95?

Q6: Will my DOS and Windows 3.1 software work under Windows 95?

Q7: What other multimedia controls does Win 95 have?

Chapter 16:   Macintosh Multimedia Madness: In the Beginning

Q1: The CD-ROMs outer box lists all these Minimum

Hardware Requirements: 68020 or higher, 256 colors, System 7, 8 megs of RAM, 10Mb hard disk space available. How do I find out what MY Mac has?

Q2: What is the difference between System 6 and System 7? Can I still run multimedia titles if my Mac has System 6 on it?

Q3: The Minimum System Requirements for the game are at least 4 Mb of RAM. About This Macintosh says I have more than 4 Mb of RAM available. I get a Not Enough Memory error when I try to play. Why?

Q4: Most games have an Installer. What exactly is it doing?

Q5: What if I don't have enough space on my hard disk for even the smallest install?

Chapter 17:   CDs and CD-ROM Drives—How to Become a Spin Doctor

Q1: I don't see the CD-ROMs icon on the desktop when I insert it.

Q2: It works if it's the only device in the chain, but not if I connect another drive.

Q3: I just changed discs, why do I still see the grayed-out icon for the previous disc?

Q4: My CD has dirt, finger prints or dust on the data surface. How should I clean it?

Q5: AARRGGHH! My disc has scratches, is there any hope?

Q6: My CD-ROM seems to read discs poorly. Can I fix this?

Q7: I bought a new Quad or Hex spin CD-ROM drive, but my programs don't seem to run any faster. Why?

Chapter 18: Sound: What Puts the Multi in Multimedia?

Q1: I hear it, but it's not very loud. How do I make it louder?

Q2: The built-in speaker is wimpy. How do I get heart-stopping sound out of my Mac? Do I need a sound card or something? What?

Q3: I don't hear anything now that I've plugged in my fancy new multimedia amplified speakers.

Q4: How do I play a music CD on my CD-ROM drive?

Q5: I'm trying to play a music CD. I've inserted the disc, opened the AppleCD Audio Player, and clicked the Play button. The elapsed time number changes but I don't hear anything.

Q6: The sounds that come out of my speakers are crackly and distorted. What can I do?

Chapter 19: Video & QuickTime: Makin' Movies Work Better

Q1: My screen flickers, or my system freezes. What should I do?

Q2: What can I do about poor picture quality?

Q3: The software runs, but my videos skip, stutter, pause or have jerky sound. How can I fix this?

Chapter 20: Memory: Things to Remember

Q1: I only have 4 (or 5) megabytes of RAM. I can't play most games without Virtual Memory or RamDoubler. But you said they may cause QuickTime movies to play back poorly.

Q2: I've disabled all unnecessary extensions and control panels and I still get a not enough memory error when I try to launch the game.

Q3: I've got lots of RAM16 (or more) megs of it. Can I use any of it to make my multimedia titles run faster?

Q4: I've increased the Preferred memory size. Now when I launch the program I receive a not enough memory error.

Q5: I can't type anything into the Preferred size box!

Q6: I don't see any of the memory things in the Info window.

Q7: I have a Power Macintosh. Anything special I should know about memory?

Chapter 21: The Final Word: A Few More Tips, Hints, and Troubleshooting Suggestions

Q1: The program crashes (freezes, bombs, quits unexpectedly, etc.) when I launch it. What is happening?

Q2: I have a quad-speed CD-ROM drive and it still seems slow to me. Anything I can do besides buy a faster drive?

Q3: Any other inexpensive ways to soup up my Mac for multimedia?

Q4: How come there are so many pages about DOS and Windows and so few pages devoted to the Mac?

Appendix C

List of Contributing Vendors

To prepare for this project, we wrote most of the multimedia software vendors we could find, requesting demonstration copies of their software, their top troubleshooting tips, and answers to common technical questions. The list that follows below contains all the vendors that responded to our requests. Please take a moment to peruse this list, and if you're shopping around for more software for your CD-ROM, feel free to consider them when deciding what you should purchase.

ABC/EA Home Software
1450 Fashion Island Blvd
San Mateo, CA 94404-2064
800-245-4525
Evals: 3D Atlas

Access
4910 W. Amelia Earhart Dr
Salt Lake City, UT 84116
800-800-4880
Evals: Under a Killing Moon

Activision
11601 Wilshire Boulevard,
Suite 1000, 10th Floor
Los Angeles, CA 90025
310-473-9200
Evals: PowerHits: Sci-Fi,
PowerHits: Movies,
PowerHits: Sports,
PowerHits: BattleTech,
Return to ZORK, Shanghai II:
Dragon's Eye, Power Game
III: Super Tetris, Spectre, F-
15 Strike Eagle, ZORK
Anthology, Atari 2600
Action Pack, Shanghai:
Great Moments, Simon the
Sorcerer

Adeline Software Int, EA
1450 Fashion Island
Boulevard
San Mateo, CA 94404-2064
415-571-7171
Evals: Relentless: Twinsen's
Adventure

Ant Software c/o Masque Publishing
PO Box 5223
Englewood, CO 80155
303-290-9853
Evals: Shadows of Cairn

Apogee Software Ltd.
PO Box 476389
Garland, TX 75047
214-278-5655
Evals: Rise of the Triad

Blizzard Entertainment
PO Box 18077
Irvine, CA 92713
714-556-6671
Evals: WarCraft: Orcs and Humans

Broderbund
PO Box 6121, 500 Redwood Boulevard
Novato, CA 94948-6121
800-521-6263
Evals: Myst, 3D Home Architect, CD-Ensemble Print Shop Deluxe

Cambium Development Inc
PO Box 296-H
Scarsdale, NY 10583
800-231-1779
Evals: Sound Choice

Casady & Greene
22734 Portola Drive
Salinas, CA 93908
408-484-9228
Evals: Conflict Catcher 3

CharisMac Engineering
66D P&S Lane
Newcastle, CA 95685
916-885-1410
Evals: CD AutoCache

Claris Clear Choice
5201 Patrick Henry Drive
Santa Clara, CA 95052-8168
Evals: From Alice to Ocean

Compton's NewMedia
2320 Camino Vida Roble
Carlsbad, CA 92009-1504
800-862-2206
Evals: The Complete MM Bible

Corel
1600 Carling Avenue, The Corel Building
Ottawa, ON, CD K1Z 8R7
800-772-6735
Evals: Clip Art Gallery 2, Images of France, Bald Eagles, Art Show 5, Worlds Best Digital Photos, CorelDRAW 5

Deep River
PO Box 9715-975
Portland, ME 04104
800-643-5630
Evals: USA Travel Guide

DeLORME
Lower Main St., PO Box 298
Freeport, ME 04032-9988
800-227-1656
Evals: Global Explorer, Street Atlas USA, Map'n'Go

The Discovery Channel
7700 Wisconsin Avenue
Bethesda, MD 20814-3579
800-762-2189
Evals: Sharks, Animal Safari

Dynamix
1600 Mill Race Drive
Eugene, OR 97403
800-757-7707
Evals: Earthsiege—
Expansion pack

Electronic Arts, Bullfrog Productions
1450 Fashion Island Boulevard
San Mateo, CA 94404-2064
415-571-7171
Evals: Magic Carpet

Expert Software
800 Douglas Road, 750
Executive Tower
Coral Gables, FL 33134-3128
800-759-2562
Evals: CD-ROM Astronomer

FWB
2040 Polk St., Suite 215
San Francisco, CA 94109
415-474-8055
Evals: CD-ROM Toolkit

Graphics Zone
38 Corporate Park
Irvine, CA 92714
Evals: Prince Interactive,
Bob Dylan Interactive

Gremlin
Carver House, 2-4 Carver Str
Sheffield S1 4FS, England

Evals: Retribution,
Slipstream 5000

HyperBole Studios
P.O. Box 2708
Seattle, WA 98111-9905
Evals: The Vortex: Quantum Gate II

I-Motion
1341 Ocean Avenue, Box 417
Santa Monica, CA 90401
800-443-3386
Evals: Chaos Control, Alone in the Dark 3

id Software, Inc.
18601 LBJ Freeway, Suite 615
Mesquite, TX 75150
800-434-2637
Evals: Heretic

Interplay
17922 Fitch Avenue
Irvine, CA 92714
714-553-6655
Evals: Descent, Cyberia,
Virtual Pool, Xplora1 Peter
Bagrielís Secret World

IVI Publishing
7500 Flying Cloud Drive
Minneapolis, MI 55344-3739
612-996-6000
Evals: Next Step Mars?,
Virtual Body, Home Medical
Advisor, Sports Health and
Fitness

Knowledge Adventure
4502 Dyer Street
La Crescenta, CA 91214
800-542-4240

Evals: Bug Adventure, Space Adventure, Dinosaur Adventure, Body Adventure, Aviation Adventure, Science Adventure, The Discoverers, Kid's Encyclopedia, Jump Start Kindergarten, My First Encyclopedia

Legend
14200 Park Meadow Drive
Chantilly, VA 22021
703-222-8500
Evals: Death Gate, Superhero League of Hoboken, Mission Critical Demo

Lifestyle Software Group
63 Orange St.
St. Augustine, FL 32084
800-289-1157
Evals: Garden Companion, Southern Living Cookbook, AstroScopes

Maxis
2 Theater Square, Suite 230
Orinda, CA 94563-3346
800-333-MAXIS
Evals: SimCity 2000

Medio Multimedia
2643 151st Place NE
Redmond, WA 98052-5562
800-788-3866
Evals: Medio CD-ROM Mag Vol. 2, Issue 3., Medio CD-ROM Mag Vol. 2, Issue 1

Microforum
1 Woodborough Avenue
Toronto, ON, CD M6M 5A1
800-465-2323
Evals: Maabus

MicroLogic Software
1351 Ocean Avenue
Emeryville, CA 94608-1128
800-888-9078
Evals: PrintMaster Gold

Microprose
180 Lakefront Dr
Hunt Valley, MD 21030
410-771-0440
Evals: Master of Magic, X-Com: Terror from the Deep

Microsoft
One Microsoft Way
Redmond, WA 98052-6399
800-426-9400
Evals: TechNet, Windows 95

Mindscape / Software Toolworks
60 Leveroni Court
Novato, CA 94949
800-234-3088
Evals: Dragon Lore, The Animals 2.0, Star Wars Chess, World Atlas, Grammys, Mavis Beacon 3, Capital Hill

Morgan Interactive
160 Pine Street, Suite #509
San Francisco, CA 94111
415-693-9596
Evals: Trivia Machine, Recess in Greece

New World Computing
PO Box 4302
Hollywood, CA 90078
818-889-5650
Evals: Hammer of the God's

Now Software
921 S.W. Washington,
Suite 500
Portland, OR 97205
503-274-2800
Evals: Now Startup
Manager/Now Utilities

ReadySoft
3375 14th Avenue, Units 7-8
Markham, ON, Canada
L3R 0H2
905-475-4801
Evals: Space Ace, Dragon's Lair

Sierra On-Line
3380 146th Place SE,
Suite 300
Bellevue, WA 98007
800-757-7707
Evals: Incredible Toon
Machine

**Simon & Schuster
Interactive**
200 Old Tappan Road
Old Tappan, NJ 07675
800-223-2336
Evals: Dictionary for Children

**SoftKey International,
Attn: Kim Barnes**
1 Athenaeum Street
Cambridge, MA 02142
800-227-5609
Evals: Body Works 4.0

Sony Electronics
3300 Zanker Road
San Jose, CA 95134
800-352-7669
Evals: Johnny Mnemonic

Sound Source Interactive
2985 East Hillcrest Drive,
Suite A
Westlake Village, CA 91362
800-877-4778
Evals: Star Wars Trilogy
CD-ROM

Spectrum Holobyte
2490 Mariner Square Loop
Alameda, CA 94501
800-695-4263
Evals: Iron Helix, Hubble
Space Telescope CD-Rom
Archive

SSI
675 Almanor Ave, Suite 201
Sunnyvale, CA 94086
408-737-6814
Evals: Ravenloft: Stone
Prophet, Forgotten Realms:
Menzoberranzan, Renegade

Star Press Multimedia
303 Sacramento Street,
2nd Floor
San Francisco, CA 94111
415-274-8383
Evals: Sports Illustrated
Multimedia Almanac 1995,
Material World

Time Warner Interactive
2210 West Olive Avenue
Burbank, CA 91506

818-295-6600
Evals: Rise of the Robots,
Hell Cab, Aegis

Trimark Interactive
2644 30th Street
Santa Monica, CA 90405-3009
310-392-3243
Evals: Air Havoc Controller

Tsunami
48677 Victoria Lane, Suite 201
Oakhurst, CA 93644
209-683-8266
Evals: Return to Ringworld,
Flash Traffic

U.S. Gold
303 Sacramento Street,
3rd Floor
San Francisco, CA 94111
415-693-0297
Evals: Dominus

**Ulead Systems c/o S&S
Public Relations**
400 Skokie Boulevard,
Suite 200
Northbrook, IL 60062
310-523-9393
Evals: MediaStudio Pro 2.0,
MorphStudio

Videodiscovery
1700 Westlake Avenue, North,
Suite 600
Seattle, WA 98109-3012
800-548-3472
Evals: Science Sleuths—
Promo

Voyager
578 Broadway, Suite 406
New York, NY 10012
212-431-5199
Evals: Poetry in Motion,
I Photograph to Remember,
A Hard Day's Night,
Dazzeloids

WarnerActive
2210 West Olive Avenue
Burbank, CA 91506-2626
818-955-9999
Evals: Chaos Engine

World Library Inc.
2809 Main Street
Irvine, CA 92714
714-660-7111
Evals: Library of the Future

Appendix D

Windows 95 Compatability

This list shows the Windows 95 compatability status for most of the software packages we evaluated (there may be as many as ten about which we couldn't find any information). This list is a shorter version of that released by Microsoft called Win95app.hlp [DRAFT, July 1995. © 1995 Microsoft Corporation].

3D Body	No problems found.
3D Home Architect	If you use a network printer, be sure to map a printer port to the network path instead of a UNC name. The program has problems redrawing captions under Windows 95.
Aegis: Guardian of the Fleet	Requires MS-DOS Mode.
Air Havoc Controller	No problems found.
Alone in the Dark 3.0	No problems found.
Animal Safari	No problems found.
Animals, The (1.0)	GPFs occur when playing certain movies.
Animals, The (2.0)	No problems found.

Astroscopes	No problems found.
Atari 2600 Action Pack	GPFs occur occasionally when closing some applications.
Aviation Adventure	ESS488 driver creates a reverberating audio echo.
Bodyworks 4.0	No problems found.
Bug Adventure	No problems found.
Cambium Sound Choice Lite	No problems found.
Cambium Sound Choice, V.1	When playing audio clips on NEC210, ticking sounds occur.
Capitol Hill	No problems found.
CD-ROM Astronomer	No problems found.
Comanche CD	Requires MS-DOS Mode, but won't allow EMM386.EXE or any TSRs in CONFIG.SYS.
Complete Multimedia Bible	No problems found.
Corel ArtShow 1.0	No problems found.
Corel Gallery 1.0	No problems found.
Corel Professional Photos	No problems found.
CorelDRAW 5.0	Make sure the network path is associated with a printer port, to print over the net work. Use Windows 95 Help for guidelines.

Cyberia	No problems found.
Death Gate	MS-DOS Mode recommended, but program fails on various computers (e.g., on ESS 688 and Aztech WA audio cards) when running in a DOS VM.
Descent	If using a SoundBlaster AWE 32 sound card during installation, program seems to stall while testing music (just takes forever to start).
Dinosaur Adventure 3.0	Can't produce digitized speech on SoundBlaster-com patible cards.
Dragon Lore	No problems found.
Dragon's Lair CD-ROM	Requires MS-DOS mode. Because of changes to Windows, do not run Dragon's Lair setup program (copies Dragon's Lair from the CD-ROM to the hard disk). Run program directly from the CD-ROM instead.
EarthSiege 1.0 CD	Requires MS-DOS Mode.
Everywhere USA Travel Guide	No problems found.
From Alice to Ocean	No problems found.
Garden Companion	No problems found.
Grammys, The	No problems found.

Hard Day's Night, A	No problems found.
Hell Cab 1.0	Screen turns black on ATI hardware using 256-color wallpaper.
Heretic 1.0	Problems (e.g., page faults) occur when quitting or when running the introduction (only on some computers).
How Your Body Works	No problems found.
Incredible Toon Machine	No problems found.
Iron Helix	No problems found.
Johnny Mnemonic	No problems found.
Library of the Future	No problems found.
Macmillan Dictionary	No problems found.
Magic Carpet 1.0	GPFs in application occur during introduction.
Map'n'Go	Error occurs during installation, but can be ignored. Program still works OK.
MapExpert 2.0 for Windows	No problems found.
Master of Magic 1.0	No problems found.
Material World	No problems found.
Mavis Beacon Teaches Typing	When program is closed with the popup menu while the window is minimized, the

	resulting dialog box is displayed off screen. This makes the program appear to stall.
Mayo Clinic Sports H & F	No problems found.
MediaStudio Pro 2.0	No problems found.
Medio Magazine	No problems found.
Morgan's Trivia Machine	Requires 256 colors. Poor MIDI sound on GRAVIS Ultrasound cards. Problems occur with some Video 7 adapters.
My First Encyclopedia	No problems found.
Myst 1.03	No problems found.
PowerHits BattleTech 1.01	Requires MS-DOS Mode, but the user must manually configure the program's properties in Windows 95.
PowerHits Movies	Requires MS-DOS Mode, but the user must manually configure the program's properties in Windows 95. Be sure to set the working directory properly.
PowerHits Sports 1.0	No problems found.
Prince Interactive	No problems found.
Print Shop Deluxe 2.0.1	No problems found.
Printmaster Gold 1.00.18	No problems found.

Random House Kid's Ency.	GPFs occur when using MIDI with Gravis Ultrasound. Screen redraw problems may also occur.
Recess in Greece	No problems found.
Relentless Twinsen's Adv.	Requires MS-DOS mode.
Renegade: Jacobs Star 1.0	Might not have sound on PAS 16. Use SoundBlaster emulation for best results.
Return to Ringworld 1.0	No problems found.
Return to Zork 1.2	Installation may cause bluescreen error messages under Windows 95 (it's OK to ignore such errors).
Rise of the Robots	Requires MS-DOS Mode.
Rise of the Triad	No problems found.
SCI/FI Power Hits 1.0	No problems found.
Science Adventure II	Requires MS-DOS Mode, but the user must manually configure the program's proper ties in Windows 95.
Shadows of Cairn	No problems found.
Shanghai II Dragon's Eye	No problems found.
Shanghai: Great Moments	No problems found.
Sharks (Discovery Channel)	No problems found.

SimCity Enhanced CD-ROM	No problems found.
Simon The Sorceror	Requires MS-DOS Mode with 512K conventional memory. User must manually configure the program properties in Windows 95.
Southern Living Cookbook	Sound doesn't work with SoundBlaster 16 and 4MB of memory. (Get more RAM!!)
Space Ace	No problems found.
Space Adventure	No problems found.
Sports Ills. MM Almanac	No problems found.
Star Wars Chess 1.1	No problems found.
Street Atlas USA	No problems found.
Terminal Velocity 1.0	No problems found.
Under a Killing Moon	Requires MS-DOS Mode.
Undersea Adventure 3.1	No problems found.
Virtual Body, The	No problems found.
Virtual Pool	Might not render properly for some video adapters. System stalls in VESA mode after exit, for computers using ATI Mach 64.
Warcraft—Orcs & Humans	GPFs occur when running in a DOS VM; program fails on Aztech Nova 16,

	SoundBlaster 2.0 and PAS 16 SoundBlaster-emulation.
World Atlas 5.0 (CD)	The printer setup dialog box fails to open when Print Setup selected from File menu.
X-Com Terror from the Deep	No problems found.

Index